DECEIT AND EXCESS IN AMERICA

How Moneyed Interests Have
Stolen America
And

How We Can Get It Back

Dave Lefcourt

authorHOUSE®

AuthorHouse™
1663 Liberty Drive
Bloomington, IN 47403
www.authorhouse.com
Phone: 1-800-839-8640

First published by AuthorHouse 4/2/2009

ISBN: 978-1-4389-4155-4 (e)
ISBN: 978-1-4389-4154-7 (sc)

Library of Congress Control Number: 2008911604

Printed in the United States of America
Bloomington, Indiana

This book is printed on acid-free paper.

DEDICATION

This book is dedicated to my wife, Gwen, who was my editor and typist, who encouraged the author to "take it one day at a time." She has been indispensable to the effort put forth and it could not have been done without her.

CONTENTS

INTRODUCTION

Deception is eating our soul. It corrupts and debases us. Whatever moral good we have stood for has been eroded by this disease. Its legacy is our resort to torture in our misapplied "War on Terrorism," exhumed out of the ruins of 9/11. The heartfelt sympathy expressed for the victims of that criminal act, which came from all over the world, has been replaced by hatred and mistrust of our motives, primarily brought about by our trumped-up war in Iraq that was based on lies, distortions, and exaggerations perpetrated by the George W. Bush administration. That war has laid bare our imperialist overreach, which the rest of the world loathes and fears. It is we who have become the main destabilizing force in the world, not the terrorists with box cutters that brought down the Twin Towers. Can we face this truth or shall we continue to deceive ourselves?

Our economic and financial meltdown is a direct result of excesses of greed and wild speculation by Wall Street's irresponsibly deceptive mortgage loan practices and the subsequent bursting of the housing bubble. This now not only grips the nation but affects the world's financial systems, and the realization sinks in that much of the turmoil in the world has been created by us. Here again, facing the truth of our culpability will not be easy. Individuals have difficulty in admitting mistakes and taking responsibility for their actions. It will be equally discomforting for our nation to admit our mistakes, while creating much of the instability we and the world are facing.

It will be especially difficult because deception runs deep in our society. The tentacles of deceit reach into our institutions, both public and private. We have government by deception, deception in business sales and marketing appeals, even war by deception. Most wealth and power is gained through deceptive practices. We are a people who have been propagandized, manipulated, and controlled by those interests that control the reins of power; all done in the name of the people. Our primary sources of information, the mainstream media (MSM), are owned and controlled by big-moneyed corporate interests. The media, television and print journalism, has been used as propaganda tools in advocating for the government's policies (particularly in the run-up to the war in Iraq), essentially abrogating its essential responsibility as a government watchdog and keeping the people informed.

Meanwhile, our excesses are legendary, from our enormous debt, both personal and national, to our bloated military budget to our rates of obesity; examples abound of our excessive behavior.

There is no way to describe every element of deception and excess that exists in America; suffice it to say, they are endemic throughout the fabric of our society.

As for the big-moneyed interests in America, all the power rests in the hands of those interests, who control the political process to the benefit of those interests and to the detriment of the of the public interest.

This is how our country, America, operates.

It is necessary to understand that what is presented here should not be interpreted as some diabolical conspiracy operating in this country. That idea must be dispelled.

Of course, there have been conspiracies of a type that have operated in this country, for example, when the Tammany Hall Society was operating in New York City early in the twentieth century; how they did "business" was a form of conspiracy (i.e., bribing politicians to vote a certain way).

Many consider the Kennedy assassination a conspiracy, and that belief still has a large following.

But what clearly needs to be established is that there is no overarching Big Brother pulling the strings, and nothing in these pages should be interpreted as such.

Did the Bush tax cuts favor the rich? Is his family not part of those that benefited? Are most of his friends, pals, cronies a part of those who shared in this bounty? Have his policies overall benefited the big-moneyed and special interests? Here again, the same positive answer.

What is put forth in these pages is the idea that there are like-minded, powerful, big-moneyed, and special interests that operate in similar ways, who assert their influence over the political agenda and the politicians they bankroll, who along with the lobbyists they hire make certain their interests are advanced. That is indirect power; those who have it and wield it are the insidious, unelected rulers who reign over this country, not acting in the public interest and certainly not to the benefit of the people.

A saying attributed to Ben Franklin describes our country this way: "A Republic, if you can keep it." Jefferson remarked, "An informed citizenry is the best defense against tyranny by the State."

Needless to say, we, as a people, have not been vigilant; our mainstream media has been less than informative, all but abandoning its role as the natural skeptic of government, evolving into an institution with scant real investigative reporting, becoming instead an enabler and triumphalist cheerleader, while performing mainly as a stenographer to government's pronouncements in its feeble attempt to maintain objectivity.

Our "Republic" has acted in imperialist, neocolonial ways: initiating a pre-emptive war and occupation; embracing secrecy (all in the name of "national security"); advocating torture; invoking warrantless wiretapping, indefinite detention, suspension of habeas corpus, and rendition to secret sites; and affirming that, in a time of war, a concept of the "unitary executive" is unaccountable and beyond congressional oversight. These are the ways of a totalitarian, imperialist dictatorship, not a "Republic." A government resorting to propaganda, fabricating and selling a case for an unprovoked, pre-emptive war with visions of a "mushroom cloud,"[1] weapons of mass destruction (WMD) in Iraq under Saddam Hussein, connected to 9/11 and al Qaeda; while in reality this

---

1   *This was said by Condoleezza Rice, as National Security Advisor, to President Bush in 2001.*

3

was a case of intimating an "imminent threat," when in fact, there was none. And it worked.

We are used to being sold, used to being beguiled and seduced. The government is no different. In the latest case, the Bush administration wanted a war with Iraq and wanted to remove Saddam Hussein. It had to sell it to the American people. Bush didn't invent these methods, but he knew they would work. Why shouldn't they work? They've worked before. The American people are prone to this sort of thing. Invoke the image of 9/11, wave the flag, spout patriotism while ridiculing and disparaging critics as unpatriotic and soft on terrorism. These are tried-and-true methods. A poll was taken prior to the onset of the war on Iraq in 2003, whereby over 70 percent of the people believed Saddam Hussein was behind the attacks of 9/11. No such evidence existed to this allegation, yet 70 percent believed it!

Majorities in every European country were against going to war in Iraq, including the people of Great Britain. Yet in the United States, the people backed going to war overwhelmingly. How could people, whose majorities are of similar heritage, and ethnic and religious backgrounds, with similar value systems, believe so differently?

Something else is working in America and not in Europe. Americans are brought up in schools where the premium is on compliance and conformity; they are bombarded with all manner of advertising, marketing, and sound bite news; and they are addicted to consumption. In essence, they are perfect foils for propaganda, the subtle and pernicious appeals intended to entice them for a desired action and convincing to a majority of the people.

One need not be paranoid or a conspiracy theorist to wonder what is in the American character that enables him to be so susceptible to the insidious propaganda to which we are subjected. Of course, it is not portrayed as such. It is presented with an aura of plausibility and believability, and if you don't think critically and question it beyond the surface, it could make sense and thus be believable. When it is repeated enough times, using various spokesmen spouting the same thing, it takes on a life of its own.

It is the same with retail advertising. One time does not do the trick, even if it is bad advertising. The idea is to get people to remember it, and what better way is there than repeating it? People hear it repeated enough, and they remember it. In time, the people believe it.

Critical thinking and questioning is the archenemy of propaganda, just as lies cannot stand up to fact. If you have an enemy that does not meet the standard of an actual, monolithic threat, then you invent one, contrive it, and make it into something it is not. That was Iraq; it was no imminent threat, it had nothing to do with 9/11, and it had no weapons of mass destruction. But it was made to "appear" as if it was all those things.

If you do not believe you are being sold a bill of goods, what you hear must be true; the lie is masked as the truth, and you believe it. This is what we have let happen in this country. We were not vigilant and did not see beyond the hype.

We have been exposed to all manner of politically correct but misleading name changes that have been promulgated upon us (e.g., the Defense Department rather than the War Department[2]; "defensive" instead of "offensive"; our armies protecting us, fighting for us, defending us instead of being used as aggressors).

There have always been propaganda and lies; "Manifest Destiny" was made to sound like the inevitable and innocent Westward expansion instead of naked aggression, stealing the land, while destroying the American Indian culture and way of life. We demonized them with they are "savages," they "scalp" people. What would you do if someone was stealing your land? Fight back? They did and they were vanquished, packed off to reservations on hard-scrabble land.

Today, the Internet is seen as a threat to the powers in control. It is uninhibited, raw, and unadulterated, pure in the sense it is not yet ruled by those who wish to control it. Therefore, it is "dangerous."

The sixties' protests were seen as a threat to the powers and institutions that ruled. The sixties were also uninhibited, exhibitionist, and revolutionary. When the protestors put the flag on the seat of their

2   *After World War II, the War Department was renamed the Defense Department.*

pants, they openly rejected the war in Vietnam and those who were precipitating it. That is why there is no draft today. "Volunteers" are more easily controllable, less open to question, more malleable.

Our "leaders" saw what developed some forty years ago and eliminated the draft. They were determined to not let that happen again. So over time, what has evolved in America is a gradual, almost imperceptible metamorphosis of those that determine the political agenda, control the levers of power, enact the laws and regulations, not in a conspiratorial concert, but with like-minded interest, and presented as "in the interests of the people." Everything doesn't have to be spelled out exactly, cross every "t," dot every "i." It is "business," and in business the decision makers do whatever they have to do to get what serves their own interests to mask their true intent while making more money and increasing their own power. Blatant, obvious control and overt police state tactics are unnecessary, as insidious, imperceptible control is better, particularly when you wrap the flag around it.

The Bush-Chaney mob got cocky; they figured they could get away with connecting everything with 9/11, their "Get out of jail free" card. The "unitary executive," we're at "war," an endless war against a shadowy "terrorist" enemy, who "hates our freedom," in their "War on Terrorism."

If there was no real enemy to fight, invent one, make it out to be something it is not and can never be, portray it as something monolithic, an imminent threat or a potential one intent on destroying you, and you must fight it to the death.

Things do not happen spontaneously, without cause. Things happen, but there is always something to cause it and bring it about.

America is the way it is from the forces (powers) that influence it, own it, manipulate it, and direct it.

Eighty percent of the American people say, "The country is off-track." Here are a few clues as to why things are the way they are and a few recommendations as to what Americans can do about it.

GOVERNMENT, LOBBYISTS, MONEYED AND SPECIAL INTERESTS

On July 29, 2008, Senator Ted Stevens (R.-Alaska) was indicted on seven counts of corruption charges by a federal grand jury, stemming from his alleged concealment of hundreds of thousands of dollars in gifts from an Alaskan oil field services company (one of the most powerful in Alaska, as reported in *The Baltimore Sun* on July 30, 2008).

Stevens allegedly accepted more than $250,000 worth of improvements on his home as well as other gifts. The "Ethics in Government Act" requires lawmakers to report any gifts in excess of certain amounts. He has since been convicted on all counts.

To suppose this is an isolated incident of a lawmaker's corruption stretches all credulity (only the most blatant get caught). The interplay of money and politics is at the heart of our system, which has big money bankrolling politicians, who are then beholden to these benefactors, who along with their lobbyists help shape the political agenda to the benefit of these big-moneyed interests. Essentially it is, "We take care of you and you take care of us." And where is the public interest in all of this? Stiffed and lied to, with deception and assorted propaganda expounded by these "leaders" onto the people they supposedly represent.

We are in trouble. Those elected have not acted in the best interests of the United States, its people, its laws, and the Constitution they swore to uphold.

This is a dangerous time in this country, especially for the middle-class working man/woman, dependent as they are on the next paycheck.

He has been enticed to spend and increase his debt, and increasingly he is in jeopardy of losing not only his job but his career.

The symbiosis of money and power is choking the American worker. Good-paying jobs with good benefits are vanishing by corporate decisions to move production to cheap-labor countries. The products produced by this labor are marketed to entice buyers by their low prices. This benefits the corporation honchos and the stockholders of this company but hardly the unemployed workers in this country who used to make those products.

And of course the consumer is complicit in this unholy enterprise by buying these "low-priced" products, thereby ensuring the further strangulation of our ever-diminishing middle class. We become the means to our own diminished status by helping the ever-widening gulf of expanding the wealth of the rich while expanding the size of the poor.

And where are our elected representatives in all this? Passing the legislation that is corporate friendly while disastrous for the American worker.

Manufacturing in this country has diminished by millions of lost jobs, primarily those with higher wage rates and benefits. This has reduced the number of middle-class people in this country.

Outsourcing is just one of the latest phenomena to diminish those jobs, while increasing the company's bottom line. The ones who suffer when this occurs are not the high-level executives who run the company. It is those caught in the middle and below them who are displaced.

Meanwhile, the U.S. government offers tax breaks to those companies who leave instead of providing tax breaks for companies to stay in the United States. There is simply no incentive to stay. The government thus becomes complicit in the demise of American jobs.

Big money and special interests dictate everything. They are behind almost every political decision. There is no real public interest. That is no more than a public relations propaganda campaign thrown out as a smokescreen by those in power to deflect from their real motives, which are to benefit themselves and their financial backers.

Take the example of the hedge fund financial wheeler-dealers and the regulation of their activities. When legislation was offered to control and regulate their financial dealings, the powerful chairman of the Senate Finance and Banking Committee, Senator Charles Schumer (D.-New York), opposed those regulatory efforts and prevented the legislation from coming to a vote. And why would such a liberal progressive senator go against what seemingly is in the public interest? Schumer did so simply because he had benefited from hedge fund largesse in the form of their supporting his campaigns for re-election.

This is a part of the dishonesty that pervades the entire political process. When Republicans or Democrats are beholden to the interests that sustain their being elected or re-elected, and retaining their power, they become a part of the corrupted system. It has been a self-perpetuating system, a revolving door that goes on largely unabated, short of occasional scandals and corruption that were so brazen and obvious(Abramoff[3]) that something had to be done, otherwise the entire unregulated system would be completely exposed and all the political perpetrators would be ensnared. So you have the sham of hearings that catch the most egregious offenders, while "self-righteous" others (equally as guilty as those they condemn) are let off the hook.

Some superficial legislation may be passed, but business as usual remains intact. Foxes in henhouses are sometimes caught, because there are some really stupid foxes. But a system that breeds and feeds on itself, in an incestuous marriage of the unscrupulous and the predatory, lives on.

Today in America, the same type of deception applies to going to war. Going to war for oil, market domination, hegemony, or empire cannot be advocated; we have to go war to protect the nation because of imminent threats of WMD, and to defend against terrorists. All to sell to a public steeped in being sold beer and cars; selling war is done the same way. Package it, depict it as, "You don't want a mushroom cloud," they are "connected to al Qaeda."[4]

---

3   *Jack Abramoff, the former lobbyist, since convicted, bribed congressmen (mostly Republicans), lavished them with vacation junkets, plying them with all sorts of goodies, until his activities were so overt they drew the attention of federal investigators, not only bringing himself down, but a number of congressmen as well.*

4   *Condoleezza Rice.*

We tend to deride corruption in many other countries, as in the petty type of payoffs to officials who grant the authority to build a building or receive the necessary approvals to do business. In cases like Afghanistan, it may take the form of paying a toll to a local warlord in order to pass on a road.

In our own country, we have romanticized the protection rackets of a bygone era in an almost nostalgic way as something in our past that we have cleaned up, that no longer exists.

Our corruption is of an insidious nature, deception on a grand scale, and we have become the complicit, often unwitting partners of the disease that is eating at our collective soul.

It is all interconnected, not a conspiracy, but a mutually beneficial alliance of like-minded interests that is lethal to our very being as a people and as a nation.

As George Carlin said of money and power, "It's an exclusive club and you're not in it."

FINANCIAL MARKETS AND THE ECONOMY

The current distress in the banking and mortgage industry was born in a climate of speculation fueled by greed in a system of deregulation and little oversight. The industry lobbied to create the system and was abetted by their subservient Congress. The complex financial schemes created were a mixture of Byzantine practices that produced enormous profits and fees while the market climbed to unsustainable heights, until it came crashing down with the bursting of the housing bubble and the orgy of bad subprime mortgage loans (that should not have been made, which encouraged reckless debt, while creating countless defaults in a domino-like effect that has no end in sight at this time.)

According to a story in *USA Today* on July 16, 2008, "The root of the economic problem remains the fallout from the imploding housing bubble."

Not true! The housing bubble is a symptom of the economic problem. The root cause lays in rampant speculation that had no effective oversight and regulation on the practices utilized by the banking and financial industry.

If there were problems in the subprime mortgage industry, they resided below the radar until the crisis fully exploded. This financial meltdown continues, which at the time of this writing, saw Lehman Brothers file for Chapter 11 bankruptcy protection and Bank of America acquire Wall Street's Merrill Lynch brokerage firm, while the Dow dropped 500 points in trading, and the meltdown is far from over.

Two days later American International Group (AIG), the insurance behemoth, with tentacles worldwide, was saved from immediate bankruptcy when the Fed issued an $85 billion "loan" to forestall its "liquidation" over the next two years. This was done to avert a calamity that could affect financial stability with worldwide economic repercussions.

With the banking industry troubles, the focus continues on stabilization and preventing greater damage, actual and psychological. The momentum clearly is heading south.

One day after the bloodbath of September 15, a *New York Times* editorial acknowledged, "It is certainly not too soon to look beyond the current crisis to the flows and fallacies of the anti-regulatory ideology that has held Washington in its grip since the Reagan years and allowed the financial excesses that are now stressing the system to the breaking point.... The nation needs a new perspective on the markets, one that acknowledges the self-destructive bent of unfettered capitalism and its ability, unchecked, to wreak havoc far beyond Wall Street."

Yet blame for the underlying causes has taken a back seat to the day-to-day reality. When the dust settles, is it likely that the root cause (wild, deregulated speculation) will be brought under tough regulations and oversight, while the foxes, the remaining big-moneyed and special interests, and a Congress that works hand and glove with them, are still in control of the agenda? Or, as usual, Bear Stearns, Lehman Brothers, and AIG, a few culprits (CEOs) will get the guillotine, a few banks and financial houses will go under, but as happened with the savings-and-loan crisis before it, real government regulation and oversight, with laws and regulations that are strictly enforced, is unlikely to occur.

The unfettered capitalists of the banking and finance industries are all too steeped in a laissez faire mindset, embracing greed and arrogant speculation to be authentically chastened and repentant by the latest financial crisis that they created and for which they are responsible.

Most of the real culprits will go unscathed. Let us take a snapshot of how the system works. Big-moneyed corporate, financial, and deep-pocketed special interests bankroll the elected officials in office, who are then beholden to them to help determine the legislative agenda to enact the laws and regulations that benefit these interests; they have ex-congressmen as lobbyists to further those interests; and they install former corporate bigwigs in regulatory capacities to oversee these industries. It is a closed system, a deregulated system whereby in a real economic meltdown, only the blatant scapegoats are caught (the demise of Bear Stearns, Lehman Brothers, and AIG) but damage control is contained by federal bailouts and Fed takeovers until the system can go back to business as usual. Government, beholden to big-moneyed corporate and special interests rather than being beholden to the people, acts to protect those interests to the detriment of the people. The people are fed propaganda, are told by the president, "These are difficult times for American families," but the real truth of why they are in this economic plight is hidden, masked in deception.

Meanwhile, no real reforms are likely to occur because the essential corruption of the system remains in place, making real reforms impossible.

When the economy was swimmingly good, there was no way people would consider change and reform. Only now with a severe economic dislocation do people care, get upset, and complain. When you are "satisfied," what is there to complain about? But when it hits home economically (e.g., mortgage crisis, high gas prices, stock losses, loss of job, credit card debt, home value below equity of the home), then the people cry out for something to be done.

Today's meltdown in the economy and financial markets with derivatives, "packaging" mortgages into funds, and other assorted financial schemes is mind-boggling; suffice it to say, people know something is not right. Reading about some financial wheeling and dealing suggests "Wild West" activity with little regulation, speculation run rampant, and obviously a lot of people getting burned badly financially. Then the Fed bails out a Bear Stearns for fear of a "bank run"; you sense this is no isolated occurrence, but just the tip of the iceberg. In the heyday of rising real estate values before the subprime mortgage loan crisis, some people were looking for the quick buck. And some vulturous lenders took advantage of some people who should not have been approved for loans in the first place. Of course, these are the people defaulting, and abandoning their properties, and going into bankruptcy.

Instituting proper regulatory practices that should have been in effect and that would have prevented such occurrences, but after the "horses are out of the barn," is a little "Katrina like," but typical of government ineptitude. You should not have to guess who will "pay the piper" on this one. You can bet it will not be the well-heeled and carnivorous sorts at the top of the food chain.

The "super rich" traders and CEOs with outlandish incomes, living in over-the-top ostentatiousness, living as modern-day kings, feeling "entitled" as they do at their ability to amass a fortune while manipulating and exploiting the financial system, are financial Attilas that lay waste as they exploit and profiteer. They do not build anything, they do not make anything, they are just new age "robber barons," the Attilas of finance profiteering exploiters, "P.I.M.P.S." (predators in market profiteering scams).

The mortgage crisis was created by largely deregulated financial interests that engaged in practices that more resembled pyramid schemes than sound financial deals.

We have trillion-dollar deficits, have profligate conspicuous consumption wholly beyond personal need, are beholden economically to foreign holders of our debt to keep the economy afloat, and are precariously propped up as a house on stilts in the middle of a hurricane.

Rome burned while Nero supposedly fiddled, a seemingly poignant way of saying how we initially responded to the crisis confronting us. We were headed for a train wreck, a day of reckoning, yet in almost complete disconnect and denial.

Americans have been in an age where hard work is equated with being a fool, where get-rich-quick schemes abound, and some of the best and brightest are enticed and drawn in to make easy money in dubious enterprises.

Former Federal Reserve Chairman Alan Greenspan referred to it as "irrational exuberance," instead of saying it is the tip of the iceberg of a system defying all rules and regulations and out of control, underwritten by the federal government, where the people not only pay the ultimate cost, but will then be blamed instead of holding the charlatans of business and finance accountable. If they were held accountable, the system would be exposed for what it is: dishonest and deceitful to the core, where the rich get off unscathed and the people are gouged.

"Have a nice day (while we take complete advantage of you!)." To the people who were sold, sealed, and delivered as so much fodder to be used and abused at will, it was as simple as apple pie.

Robert Scheer, the editor of the "Truth Dig" blog, wrote in his July 29, 2008, article, "Sucking up to the Bankers: A Bipartisan Lovefest": "This is a time to condemn the bankers, not to embrace them. They are the scoundrels who got us into the biggest economic mess since the Great Depression, lining their own pockets while destroying the life savings of those who trusted them. Yet both of our leading presidential candidates are scrambling to enlist not only the big-dollar contributions but, more frighteningly, the 'expertise' of the very folks who advocated the financial industry deregulations at the heart of this meltdown."

Scheer went further to add that during the Clinton administration, legislation was passed empowering "the banking bandits." This resulted from Clinton Treasury Secretary Robert Rubin's critical support of the Gramm-Leach-Bliley Act in 1999 (which essentially deregulated the banking and financial industry, which is at the root cause of today's financial crisis). It was reciprocated within days of its passage when Rubin was given a top job worth $15 million a year at Citibank (a main benefactor of this legislation).

Dean Baker, an economist and co-director at the Center for Economic and Policy Research (CEPR) in Washington, D.C., was prescient when he wrote *on January 18, 2005* (as cited in TomPaine.com), "The collapse of the stock bubble in 2000 was difficult enough, but the housing bubble collapse—and there will be one—will be even worse. Why? Because housing wealth is more evenly distributed than stock, meaning many more middle and low-income families will be affected. Those who have borrowed against their homes will have the toughest time. Our country's leaders have let things get this bad. Now, regular Americans will deal with the consequences.

"This will be especially hard on families who have borrowed heavily against their homes, particularly those close to retirement" as "the ratio of home equity to mortgage debt is at a record low. As a result, millions of families will be hard hit by a sharp drop in home prices, in many cases finding their mortgage debt exceeds the value of their home."

This was all created by the deregulated, greedy banking and financial speculators, who engaged in practices and schemes that bilked the system by successfully lobbying their elected cohorts in Congress, who enacted the laws and regulations that gave speculators free rein.

CORPORATISM: FRANCHISING, MONOPOLIZATION, MARKETING, AND ADVERTISING

The large corporate, franchised enterprise has become endemic in America and is omnipresent in our daily lives (TV, ads, news). What we buy, where we shop, what we see and hear in the public sphere is corporate, franchised speak and logo omnipresent. It infects everything.

The merchandising and marketing appeal of the corporations serves to undermine critical thinking in favor of mass appeal as it dampens vibrant and creative thought. Large corporate enterprises' deceptive methods stunt the imagination with the banality of marketing sloganeering.

The appeal of merchandising and marketing is enticing and addicting. Its essence is nothing more than to gain power and profit, irrespective of the propaganda's "by-products." The by-products' casualties are rampant obesity, drug addiction, crime and incarceration, shopping addiction: a nation of users and consumers.

Americans have been on an orgy of excess. Look at the size of houses built, the size of vehicles driven, the amount of debt accumulated, the amount of food consumed, the amount of energy used. The amount spent on food, clothing, and shelter is conspicuously beyond basic needs.

Somehow the concept of having enough and being satisfied has been lost by many American people (maybe the same with exaggerations and lies). If these Americans cannot recognize the difference between when they are filled and when they need to eat, perhaps they have lost the ability to distinguish the difference between reality and what is imaginary, what is the truth and what is a lie.

Advertisers keep marketing their wares. Advertisers believe the people can be lured into buying something and that need has nothing to do with it. Advertisers entice people to believe they want it; they just do not know they want it yet. When the people hear it over and over, they wonder, "Maybe I do need it."

America's consumer spending has become the primary engine of our economy. Promoting that spending is one of the hand-and-glove purposes of government and business. Yet, spending and consuming has gone beyond all need and has created excess, reflected in consumer debt.

Many Americans have more than one credit card, and they are enticed to get others, to use them until the cards are maxed out and the card owners are forced to pay exorbitant usury fees while they sink deeper and deeper into debt. Add in the second mortgages, home equity loans, and now the decline in home values, and many are in economic crisis. Concomitantly, there is the urgent need to rein in deregulated business and financial practices that fueled this orgy.

The accountability should be mainly on the promoters of this financial ruin and not on the consumers who have been bilked and manipulated by the unscrupulous in suits and ties.

Maybe some people became lost in our sea of plenty, their values somehow distorted and their sense and purpose no longer clear.

Meanwhile, our governmental and business "leaders" have acted with hubris and wanton arrogance, while their deception and unrestrained business practices have given rise to any number of personal and societal maladies ("by-products" of our system).

Here then are some of those "by-products" that are related directly or indirectly to our deceptive and excessive practices creating dysfunction in our political, cultural, societal, business, corporate, and financial institutions.

- Rampant obesity

- Epidemic drug addiction

- Debt is excessive: personal, business, financial, and federal.

- We are addicted to all manner of conspicuous consumption (beyond all need).

- Manufacturing is in decline, jobs are decimated and lost.

- Jobs are outsourced.

- Small towns are dying through large corporate omnipresence and the elimination of locally owned and operated businesses.

- Mortgage loan crisis resulted from wild speculation.

- There is no health insurance for over 50 million people.

- There is a decline of the middle class and an increase in poverty rates.

- There is wide income disparity between rich and poor.

- Terrorism is widespread.

- Our government sanctions torture, indefinite detention, and rendition (surrendering a captive to a country where it is known he will be tortured).

- Our government has a policy of pre-emptive war.

- Our government encourages war profiteering.

- Unjustified defense expenditures relative to today's reality.

- There are phony "wars" on drugs and terrorism.

- There is a corporate takeover of the mainstream media.

- Our infrastructure has deteriorated through neglect.

- Our government is incompetent and dysfunctional.

- Our incarceration rates are greater than any other industrialized democracy.

- Public schools are declining from "dumbing down" the curriculum with expectations toward the lowest common denominator.

- Gambling is expanding throughout the country.

- There is rampant illegal immigration, with political partisanship preventing any solution.

Basically, what has been perpetrated on the people of this country is that big business of this country is good for America. However, when we look at some of the modern business practices of big business—corporate franchising and "Big Box" store enterprises—the picture becomes one of deception, exploitation, and monopolization.

For example, there is just no way local, small retail businesses can compete with the large franchised operations underwritten by deep-pocketed corporate parents.

The franchises can withstand declines in the economy, where declines in profits can be offset by corporate tax write-offs. Local, small businesses require a profit just to survive. Franchises can also buy in bulk and in some cases sell products at cost (or even at a loss) to lure in customers. Local businesses do not have the resources to buy in such large quantities and must sell items above costs and at a profit.

Franchises have the benefit of "name recognition." With the U.S. population as mobile as it is, people are "familiar" with franchised operations, tending to go with what they "know" rather than taking a chance with an unfamiliar name. Thus, vendors in airport terminals are mostly nationally franchised operations, and roadside restaurants and retail outlets adjacent to the nation's highways are also franchises of the big national corporations. Couple this with road bypasses around towns and cities, and small-town local retail is all but gone.

Add in the invasion of the Big Box stores selling products anywhere from food and drugs, to apparel, house-ware, and appliances in a "convenient one-stop shopping," and small towns' local businesses have all but vanished.

There is little local ownership of business anymore. This is, after all, not a new phenomenon, but one that started after World War II.

There has hardly been an industry in the Unites States that has not been affected. Big business's franchised operations have a voracious appetite for expansion, market share, and profit. It has no social responsibility, despite its public relations advertising that purports to serve the public's interest, which really just masks its one and only motive: profit.

Corporate public relations is window dressing and deceptive propaganda, made to appear to be in the public interest and to benefit the American people through corporate charitable donations, sponsorship of civic organizations (e.g., the Rotary, Lion's Club, etc.), and advertising low prices and "you get your way"—all to persuade, sell, and convey a portrayal of innocence, but hiding their real nature.

The capitalist model in the United States has survived and thrived by convincing people that low prices are beneficial to them without their realizing the consequences. Low prices killed industries in this country, killed the jobs of their neighbors, killed small-town businesses, brought with it dead-end jobs with minimum wages, and contributed to the widening disparity of incomes between corporate management and the workers.

This American capitalist model has developed a consumer culture of buying beyond all sense of need. If people were to buy on need, this house of cards would come crashing down. This system is sustained by foreign cheap labor, and our consumer culture is maintained on the backs of that cheap labor.

It is a system of basic inequality and exploitation that is mostly hidden from the American public.

Recently, some of the consequences of the Big Box store invasion were exposed by Robert Greenwald's documentary film, *Wal-Mart: The High Cost of Low Prices*. Here are some excerpts from that film.

Local resident:

"They come in to a community and force everybody else out." It is an "empty town. Looks like a neutron bomb hit it."

Lee Scott (CEO of Wal-Mart):

"Our policy is we pay for every hour worked."

Commentator (speaking to employee who refused to identify himself): "No overtime is allowed. They work off the clock. If they don't do it, they fear for their job."

Lee Scott:

We're "looking out for the environment."

Local environmental resources enforcement officer, Catawba River Valley, Charlotte, North Carolina:

They are "storing herbicides and pesticides in parking lots. Some are broken and washing into storm water system," that eventually ends up "into the public drinking water system."

Lee Scott:

"The Wal-Mart model works. Wal-Mart has a responsibility to society."

Judge (hearing case brought against Wal-Mart):

There is a "pattern of deception ... a pattern of obfuscation."

Honest competition should be the lifeblood of a true capitalist system. When business practices and actions destroy competition, particularly from unfair business practices such as receipt of monies through government actions (e.g., depletion allowances and direct subsidy), this is not capitalism, but a form of corporate welfare, where government and business act in unison to the detriment of the public interest.

This is not good for America or Americans.

GOVERNMENT, EXECUTIVE, LEGISLATIVE

As Jefferson said, "An informed citizenry is the best defense against tyranny by the State."

The George W. Bush administration has used terms such as "freedom and democracy" and has even suggested "eliminating tyranny in the world."

Yet in the George Bush administration's "War on Terrorism," it has resorted to torture, indefinite detention, suspension of habeas corpus, rendition of suspects, and warrantless wiretapping, and it initiated a pre-emptive war against an adversary that was not an imminent threat, had no weapons of mass destruction (as alleged), and had no connection to the terrorist attack on 9/11.

A democracy is built on trust.

America's greatest enemy is not terrorism or anything from without. America's greatest enemy is from within, when facts are manipulated by deception and exaggeration. American democracy is at risk when its leaders blatantly resort to propaganda in misleading its people.

All presidents and their administrations have lied from time to time, disguised and deceived, pretended not to notice and ignored criticism. However, the Bush administration has taken this behavior to new heights in its blatant use of propaganda.

Back in another day, when this country was mired in the Vietnam War, there was a senator from Oregon, Wayne Morse, who in today's jargon spoke "truth to power."

While appearing on *Face the Nation*, Morse objected to his questioner, Peter Lisagor, who said: "Senator, the Constitution gives to the president of the United States the sole responsibility for the conduct of foreign policy."

The senator responded sharply: "Couldn't be more wrong. You couldn't make a more unsound legal statement than the one you have just made. This is the promulgation of an old fallacy that foreign policy belongs to the president of the United States. That's nonsense."

Lisagor prodded him, "To whom does it belong then, Senator?"

Morse did not miss a beat: "It belongs to the American people.... And I am pleading that the American people be given the facts about foreign policy."

Lisagor persisted, "You know, Senator, that the American people cannot formulate and execute foreign policy?"

Morse became indignant. "Why do you say that?" he demanded. "I have complete faith in the ability of the American people to follow the facts if you'll give them. And my charge against my government is we're not giving the American people the facts. For where has been the trust, the forthrightness, even the idea of the need for the people to be fully informed by those who govern over them in their name?"

Today, Americans are treated like children instead of being informed of the truth. Americans are not respected as adults who can think critically when the facts are clearly laid out and which they are able to understand and to offer their judgment and assessment.

Another statement by Morse that should resonate with people today is, "We're going to become guilty, in my judgment, of being the greatest threat to the peace of the world. It's an ugly reality, and we Americans don't like to face up to it."

Senator Morse said that some forty years ago. His words ring true today.

Dissemble (to deceive) is a term that perfectly describes what the George W. Bush administration has been all about: propaganda, misinformation, outright lying, deception, cronyism, corruption, incompetence, ignoring the rule of law, presidential imperiousness with signing statements effectively gutting the law; basically, the Bush administration is all but a dictatorship with the trappings of a representative democracy masking its true character.

The Constitution has been trampled, all but ignored, as the separation of powers and congressional oversight have withered. Save for a Democratically controlled Congress since the 2006 elections and a few hearings highlighting the Bush administration's malfeasance, the idea of the "unitary executive" (professed by his administration) all but declared in a time of war he had the power and authority to do anything and Congress had no authority to rein him in.

Call it anything you want, but that's a dictatorship.

The mainstream media and their pundits (including former generals, some of whom have admitted they intentionally misled the public and now regret it) were the enablers, dissemblers, and triumphalists (in the run-up to the Iraq War and its aftermath) to the Bush follies of deceit, propaganda, and sleight of hand more reminiscent of the Kremlin during the Soviet era.

The enablers, the fawning press, were stenographers of all of the Bush administration's bleatings; the Bush crowd played them like a fiddle. You say it; we print it as objective "news" with no other views that could at least present a contrast (opposition), thereby making the "news" nothing more than a propaganda organ for the administration. What independent press?

Apologists were led by a compliant Congress (dutiful sycophants, obedient as a herd of sheep) that ignored its oversight function as a separate branch of government, repudiating its Constitutionally mandated duty as a check and balance to the executive branch as representatives of the people, and acted more as the "Duma" (the former "People's Assembly" in the U.S.S.R.) to the dictator.

And finally, the Bush administration itself, from the president and vice president on down, dissembled the truth, became myth makers of reality, allegiant to their own ideology, embraced the idea of the "unitary executive," ignored the law directly (by bypassing the FISA court), and issued "signing statements" (that part of the law it would not follow), initiated illegal detentions of suspects and rendition of detainees (with their subsequent torture, by surrogate countries like Egypt), and suspended habeas corpus in defiance of the rule of law.

In order to further understand the deceptive nature of our system, it is necessary to recognize the effect the big-moneyed financial and special interests exert in their underwriting of political candidates (our existing officeholders, particularly members of Congress as well as the main presidential candidates).

Their motivation could be hidden, as is done with the American Israel Public Affairs Committee (AIPAC), which does not fund candidates directly, but enlists deep-pocketed individuals to give directly, which obscures AIPAC's political involvement. Make no mistake, the "hidden hand" of AIPAC is there with candidates and existing officeholders "paying their respects" to the "Don" of special interest groups, whose power over the political landscape is supreme. The candidates—both presidential and congressional candidates—address the AIPAC convention and vow their undying devotion and support of Israel—the sine qua non requirement of any officeholder in the United States, it being political suicide to criticize the group, its activities, and its tactics of branding all critics as anti-Semitic. Former President Carter was widely condemned by AIPAC and its right-wing sympathizers for his book, *Palestine: Peace, Not Apartheid*, which was critical of Israel's policies in their treatment of the Palestinians in the occupied territory of the West Bank.

The art of deceptive propaganda starts with plausibility; it has to sound true or appear to be the truth. In the case of selling the idea for war with Iraq, it was presented as dire. Saddam had weapons of mass destruction; he was connected to 9/11; he could supply those weapons of mass destruction to al Qaeda terrorists.

We know now that none of these assertions were true. But at the time, President Bush, Vice President Cheney, Secretary of State Colin Powell, and the chief advisor to the president, Condoleezza Rice, made those assertions. The mainstream media dutifully reported these assertions in the newspaper, on Sunday news programs, and in the now-infamous Powell charade to the United Nations just prior to the invasion of Iraq in March 2003.

Those who act deceptively want a certain outcome. In the case of going to war in Iraq, Bush wanted the American people to believe and support his administration. Not to act would have been calamitous, as in, "You do not want a mushroom cloud," as Condoleezza Rice said.

As was said earlier, deception is endemic throughout the social fabric of America. Americans are sold to, marketed, and expected to think and act predictably (and not to think critically). The people buy even when there is no need from the same corporate, franchised stores. The people see the same advertisements, read the same mainstream media stories, see the same mainstream media talking heads, see the same mass-produced movies at the same multiplex theatres, and eat the same foods at the same corporate, franchised restaurants. It has the effect of producing a uniformity of popular cultural enterprises while marginalizing independent stores, theatres, and restaurants, and has a homogenizing effect on the culture. We may be black, brown, or white; Americans are all exposed to the same things. What is wanted is predictability, thinking and acting similarly, limiting the choices within the limited range made available. And the beauty is, many people think they are free to choose. Sure, free to choose within the range of limited possibilities made available by the same corporate, monopolized enterprises.

It is not that difficult to sell to a mass culture that is exposed to the same predictable, monopolized, and controlled enterprises. Americans are packaged and sold just like the goods they buy, the food they eat, the places they go, and the ads they see. The people are looked at as just another commodity, bought and sold, packaged and gift-wrapped.

The political power structure operates in this deceptive manner. Again, it is big-moneyed corporate and special interests that bankroll the politicians in office, who are then beholden to those interests and, together with their lobbyists, develop the political agenda that benefits those big-moneyed interests.

The lobbyists are well connected; many are former senators or congressmen, who now represent these interests to "grease the wheels" to enact the laws and regulations to benefit their clients.

The public interest is secondary except in times of national disaster (Katrina, Midwest flooding, California wildfires, infrastructure collapses such as bridges) when ignoring such events would be politically disastrous. Schools, health care, environment, infrastructure repair and maintenance, and the like are thus subordinated to the agenda of the moneyed special interests.

The deceptiveness is, these interests are not elected, yet they are the real power that reigns and rules in our system. And so it is with a mostly passive indifference by most American people that these moneyed interests and their elected handmaidens prevail, acting with impunity, arrogance, and disregard, particularly to those they supposedly represent.

As with many problem situations in this country, big-moneyed special interests are usually behind it or they want things to remain as they are and therefore are neglected. Any law, any regulation, any policy, in fact anything of any consequence, with minor exceptions (e.g., Social Security), is controlled by what big money wants, with a preference for as much deregulation as possible, along with reduced taxes and government subsidy directed toward them.

Through consolidation, monopoly, and with unlimited power, moneyed special interests do what they want.

For the United States of America, owned and operated by big money, what better than to have a conditioned and conformist-minded people doing their bidding and propagandized to believe it is in the people's interest. This is the diabolical, deceptive nature of those who reign in this country, exemplified by the imperious power of the Bush administration.

After years of being oblivious to the propaganda spewed out by the Bush administration, a majority of the people overwhelmingly rejected it; the people finally caught up to the rest of the world, which saw early on the true diabolical nature of the Bush administration.

Traditionally, these are ways of authoritarian dictatorships, fascist-type governments in league with big-business interests: militarism, religion, patriotism, and the use of nationalistic symbols (e.g., the flag), with outright suppression of dissent. These are not the ways of democratic republics. Couple the institutional control with imperialism and neocolonialism, and such a country ceases to be a republic.

The United States at present has the façade of representative democracy, which belies its true nature as a country of rich, like-minded, big-moneyed special interests that essentially control the reins of power. *This is not a conspiracy*, but big-moneyed special interest groups with like-minded desires, aims, expectations, and goals.

President Bush went to war, and the military fought it with the war equipment made by the military/industrial complex, which diabolically contributes to the country's economic growth. Thus, war making becomes a "growth" industry of economic "benefit."

Is war necessary to sustain the U.S. economy? This can't be said openly as such, but the reality is, war stimulates the economy.

As has been said, "All politicians lie," and all presidents lie.

Yet, during the early days of the Great Depression in 1933, when Franklin Roosevelt appealed to the people and said, "There is nothing to fear but fear itself," he was believed. There was a truth to what he said and people believed him. When we were attacked on December 7, 1941, there was no mistaking the enemy.

The evidence was unmistakable. So too, after the terrorist attacks on 9/11, the subsequent retaliation against al Qaeda in Afghanistan was justified; we were going after the perpetrators. Conversely, there was nothing that could justify the invasion of Iraq that remotely resembled an attack posing as an imminent threat to the United States. Only convoluted, unrelated, unconnected justifications were concocted by the Bush administration to justify this war.

This was a marked, fundamental departure in policy and was in direct refutation of international law enshrined in the United Nations, of which the United States is a charter member, stating clearly, you can only act in self-defense and where there is an imminent threat.

No country can commit an obvious lie, in defiance of the world community of nations, and be respected and trusted. Luckily, the world saw Bush's folly in Iraq as separate from the American people. It will take a new president and a new administration to try to repair the nation's standing as a country that adheres to the international standards of law and not be a rogue elephant nation, going its own way, forcing itself on others in some self-proclaimed exhortation of self-righteousness (spreading democracy and ridding the world of tyranny).

In a bipolar world (as in the cold war between the United States and the U.S.S.R.) of fairly equal adversaries and both possessing great nuclear arsenals, a standoff of "mutually assured destruction" (MAD) dictated the peace.

In the unipolar world of today, there are no real threats to American military superiority. Yet America's actions convey a threat (terrorism), which exposes the United States' insecurity, belying our superiority. Even though America is unchallenged, we act as if we are challenged. Instead of feeling secure in America's obvious military superiority, we remain suspicious of others, threatened by others, often without real foundation (Iran). Instead of promoting stability in the world, U.S. policies often exacerbate conflicts, sparking greater instability.

Secure, mature adulthood supposes an inner strength and confidence, while experience conveys a solid, thoughtful adult.

Just as with individuals, countries that are highly developed, mature, representative democracies with military superiority should be secure in this reality and act with restraint, perspective, and inner strength. They should perform a strong and confident diplomatic facilitative function in striving for stability and advocating justice as their primary focus in solving disputes and conflicts in the world.

The U.S. system of freedom and democracy and adherence to the rule of law has become corrupted to the core. A natural disaster, Hurricane Katrina, exposed decaying infrastructure (roads, bridges, levees, railroads) and the government's complete inability to respond effectively with any semblance of competence. This was appalling, laying bare the nature of what our system has become.

The American system is all of one piece, not in a conspiratorial sense, but that is why it is so insidiously deceptive. Actual dictatorships (Hitler's Nazi Germany, Stalin's Soviet Union, Pol Pot's Cambodia, and Kim Jong-il's North Korea) are easily detectable as such. In the United States, moneyed power and influence is hidden.

Such was George Bush in "liberating" the Iraqi people, "freeing" them from the oppression of Saddam Hussein. This was a snake oil dealer in the White House, a charlatan who successfully duped the American people. Bush played the people like a fiddle, and the people were duped, just as the children were led to the Pied Piper.

All countries have blood on their hands when weaker foes are vanquished by a stronger opponent. Human history is littered with empires that rose, reigned, and then fell.

We Americans, with our "exceptionalism," our sense of "entitlement," and now our military superiority, believe we are somehow "special" and can reign supreme. This arrogance and hubris is born of ignorance of history and belief in the inferiority of other peoples—their civilizations, cultures, and values. Ironically, America does not like "foreign," even though the United States is a nation of immigrants.

Are Americans the only ones who hate to face reality and the truth? Or is it a human trait to want to avoid it? Maybe being in denial is in the human genes. The truth can be discomforting. Someone is dying of inoperable cancer, and we say, "It will be all right." People talk as if eating right and exercising will make us live forever. People age; botox may remove the wrinkles, but it won't cancel inevitable death. Death is the part of life people avoid talking about, as if avoiding all talk of death will make it disappear. Death is too somber for our happy-faced, "Have a nice day" society.

Maybe Americans really are about sleight of hand.

We have never really openly acknowledged our checkered past. The same can be said for our complicity in slavery. Would open admission of guilt invalidate us as a nation? Or would it begin to cleanse the stain of our ruthless and racist past?

Saying, today, we were not part of that past ignores the truth that we are the benefactors of that past; to deny it makes us accomplices. Can we Americans, as a people, honestly face this truth?

So the Bush administration's lying and deceit follows our less-than-honorable tradition.

When the supposedly "legitimate" investment firm, Bear Stearns, went under, it was initially presented as an isolated happenstance. It was just the tip of the iceberg as the most visible failure in a deregulated, Byzantine financial structure. The financial rescue by the Federal Reserve may have prevented a "run on the banks," but the rescue did not rectify the rules and regulations that permitted a Bear Stearns to operate as it did, while at the time still permitted other firms to continue their operation as if nothing happened. To believe Bear Stearns was somehow an isolated rogue operation that was snared is similar to believing the noncommissioned officers at Abu Ghraib prison in Iraq acted as rogue torturers, as if nobody else "up the food chain" was responsible for "cutting them loose."

Abu Ghraib and Bear Stearns have nothing in common except they expose how the country has been led. When there are few regulations and lax enforcement of what rules there are, you have the makings of lawlessness. If only those who get caught are held to account and there is a failure to investigate the people and the structure that perpetrated this system, you have a cover-up of the higher-ups by a corrupt system that promotes the lawlessness that we have all too readily seen.

So many things are "out of whack."

We Americans have had a society where avoidance of responsibility is paramount. In politics, this takes the form of never admitting to anything, particularly any wrongdoing or suspect behavior.

Add in a little obfuscation, dissemble whenever there are attempts to pin down facts, and the questioner winds up frustrated and muttering.

People sense that the direction of the country is "off-track." The economy is bad; there is a mortgage loan crisis, an endless war, and gas prices at $4.00 a gallon; yet there is little agreement of the crimes that have been committed in our name.

We have not been vigilant and have let ourselves be manipulated and misled, when we should have been more skeptical and questioning. It is only now that we register our complaint and dissatisfaction, *after* the wreckage has been wrought, while we deny our own meek complicity with it.

TERRORISM, 9/11, DEATH OF COMMUNISM

Terrorism has to be kept in perspective. As former Senator Bob Kerrey(D Nebraska) of the 9/11 Commission testifying before the House Intelligence Committee on Tuesday, August 3, 2004 said,"Terrorism is a tactic." It is a method to inflict deadly harm on as many people as possible and cause as much physical damage as possible. Terrorists act in the shadows. They have no vast armies, no people, no countries they need to defend or protect.

A terrorist's aim is to undermine the sense of personal security. As for the terrorism of Osama bin Laden, he uses the technique of identifying some legitimate grievance, like U.S. troops in Saudi Arabia (since removed), or U.S. support for Arab dictatorships such as Musharraf in Pakistan (recently resigned), Mubarak in Egypt, or Saddam in Iraq; then bin Laden couples that with the Koran's (Islam's holy book) idea of Jihad and distorts it, ignoring the part about working toward personal renewal, while emphasizing the part of fighting against infidels, and defending Islam. There is nothing in Islam or the Koran that advocates *offensive* aggressive action. 9/11 was presented as an act against U.S. imperialism, attacking the infidel, and defending Islam. Many Muslims felt sympathy for bin Laden in the falling of the Twin Towers because they felt bin Laden was standing up against the oppressor, America (which supports the dictatorships that oppress the Muslims in Islamic countries).

But 9/11 was an aggressive, criminal act of terrorism. That criminal act of terrorism cannot be defended as anything else. But if the people see pictures of innocent Arab babies (as bin Laden does) killed by American bombs (or Israeli bombs), it is easy for bin Laden to make the case to oppressed Muslims that America and Israel are the enemy and, by implication, against Islam, whereby doing anything to kill that enemy becomes a defense of Islam. Thus, terrorists' acts become defending Islam. What is ignored is the distinction of these acts being aggressive and offensive in nature, specifically forbidden in the Koran.

The same can be said of the terrorist act of suicide bombing. In the Koran, suicide is also strictly forbidden. But if the enemy (America, Israel, or any of its allies) is painted and shown as the enemy of Islam, doing *anything* to defend Islam (the act that is clearly stated in the Koran) as the duty of every Muslim (with a little embellishment of a hundred virgins waiting for him in paradise after he commits the suicide bombing, as well as the suicide bomber's whole family being subsidized for his act), this is convincing to some Muslims. The specifically forbidden part of suicide is overlooked, and the martyrdom rewarded with eternal paradise for defending Islam becomes the overriding belief and the incentive to commit the act, otherwise forbidden.

Terrorists do not have planes, ships, missiles, or a large standing army at their disposal to fight the enemy, so they use what is available: cars, trucks, nails, ball bearings, a little plastic explosive, and a willing Jihadist who believes he is doing something heroic and, in the ultimate, defending Islam.

If you add the pictures of Americans humiliating and torturing Muslims (as were taken at the Abu Ghraib prison in Iraq and shown to the world and readily available on the Internet), it is not difficult to secure Muslim recruits with an almost unlimited supply, eager to fight against Islam's enemies, even to commit the act of suicide.

There is no such thing as winning the "War on Terrorism." Retaliating against terrorist acts only exacerbates the situation and causes more terrorist acts. A terrorist act is a *criminal* act and should be dealt with as such, and the perpetrators must be seen as criminals and brought to justice, as is done with any other criminal activity. Just like crime in general, terrorism will never be completely eradicated. One just has to use normal law enforcement measures, cooperate with and exchange intelligence information with cooperative governments, thereby controlling it and containing it legally. The rule of law must be adhered to and strictly followed by legitimate law enforcement.

We need some deep reflection of our existing policies of using the CIA's clandestine methods that have brought on coups of legitimate governments (Iran in 1953,[5] Chile in 1968,[6] and Vietnam in 1963[7]). We need to rethink our military bases all over the world (which is a source of deep anti-American sentiment by the local populations). We need to reconsider our hegemonic practices of supporting dictatorships, the demonizing of countries as part of some nonexistent "axis of evil" (Iraq, Iran, and North Korea). We need to reverse our policies of advocating pre-emptive aggressive wars and occupations (Iraq) and denouncing other countries that seek nuclear weapons (Iran, North Korea), while maintaining the largest nuclear arsenal and threatening to use it (nuclear "bunker busters" were talked about in going after Osama bin Laden as well as destroying Iran's nuclear facilities). We need to reverse our policy of forgoing diplomacy as an act of appeasement, thus forcing our antagonists to pursue policies to protect themselves (North Korea, Iran), particularly after seeing what the Bush administration did in pre-emptively attacking non-nuclear Iraq under Saddam Hussein.

The United States, by its policies and actions, is a primary catalytic, instigating factor in initiating and exacerbating modern-day terrorism in the world. Our policies (clandestine and overt) have contributed to the creation of Islamic terrorism. We are not facing the truth of our own culpability.

If we go back through recent history, the last seventy-five years, there were three mortal threats: Nazi Germany under Hitler, the Empire of Japan, and the Soviet Union.

---

5 *The legitimate, elected government of Iran led by Prime Minister Mossedeigh was overthrown by a coup (in 1953) instigated and carried out by the CIA with the assistance of British intelligence. It helped to install the Shah Pahlavi onto the Peacock Throne, whose oppression of the Iranian people (while in close alliance with the Americans) helped precipitate the takeover of the American Embassy and the subsequent Iranian Revolution in 1979.*

6 *The legitimately elected Allende (socialist) government was overthrown by clandestine means, led by the CIA, and a subsequent coup led by the head of the Chilean Army, General Pinochet, was installed to power with strong alliance with the United States.*

7 *The Diem government of South Vietnam was overthrown in a coup led clandestinely by the CIA.*

Hitler had visions of world domination, was working on the development of nuclear weapons, and could have succeeded in his plans if not for the overwhelming, superior firepower and war production in the West (primarily the United States), and the ability of the Soviet Union to sustain enormous casualties (20 million dead in the war), which created two war fronts. If Hitler had maintained his 1940 nonaggression pact with Stalin (instead of invading the Soviet Union), the war with Germany could well have had a different outcome.

Imperial Japan had expansionist visions of domination in Southeast Asia and had limited success. Though the attack on Pearl Harbor brought the United States into the war, Japan had no chance of winning.

The Soviet Union, having a vast arsenal of nuclear weapons and capabilities equal to the United States in firepower, was checked in its ability to use those weapons by MAD, "mutually assured destruction." Neither superpower would risk first use of these weapons, knowing their own demise would be assured in overwhelming mass retaliation. Thus the cold war of forty years ended with the breakup of the U.S.S.R. in 1991.

Today, there are no mortal threats of this magnitude anywhere in the world. Terrorism, even of Osama bin Laden's stripe, does not rise to that level of mortal threat.

Let's be clear. There is no cabal of terrorists, united in solidarity under one leader. There are many disparate groups who may identify with some of the ideas of an Osama bin Laden, but the groups are not under bin Laden's total command or direction.

It is cold war thinking, linking all "terrorists" as if they are some identifiable enemy colossus that threatens world peace, labeling and grouping all manner of insurgents, rebels, and anti-government groups into one convenient but misapplied entity. The Bush administration's phony "War on Terrorism" is a false perception promoted through propaganda and sold to the public. Thus 9/11 was equated with the Japanese attack on Pearl Harbor, and Osama bin Laden was viewed as a Hitler type with imperial ambition. This was pure hyperbolic exaggeration.

By perpetrating and perpetuating these falsehoods, we justify preemptive war, while maintaining huge, unnecessary military expenditures that make for endless war.

Where are the truth tellers who can cut through this fog of deceit and deception?

As was said earlier, terrorism is a tactic. One does not make war against a tactic. We must devise methods and ways to deal with terrorism using intelligence to disrupt and (if possible) prevent it from being carried out, undermine terrorism by supporting and supplying some of the basic needs of the people who are directly effected by terrorist excesses (as was done in Iraq with the "awakening" movement, which has many Iraqi Sunnis turning against their former Jihadist terrorist allies), and supporting justice, a true desire of all people everywhere.

We must refrain from measures that exacerbate terrorism, such as the killing of innocents, torture, rendition, and illegal detention, all reactionary measures that expand the terrorist's influence.

Most important is the sharing of intelligence with all agencies of cooperating governments to disrupt terrorist activities and to contain it. Terrorism is essentially immune from eradication, as it is like a virus to be treated, controlled, and contained; it cannot be cured.

The day of large, massed armies deployed against each other is essentially over. We are still fighting the last war, using the same methods, in the dissimilar struggles of today. It doesn't work, its costs are bloated and unnecessary, and it is a failure.

Terrorism has always existed in one form or another throughout human history. It is the tactic of the weak to confront the superior forces that oppress them. It succeeds when these superior forces overreact and create greater repression. It particularly fails in advanced democratic societies, where the actions of the terrorists are kept in perspective, calm is quickly restored as soon as possible, while the security measures are broadened, but civil liberties are maintained and overreaction kept to a minimum.

If Americans paint all adversaries as terrorists, with no recognition of those who have legitimate grievances and are oppressed by their governments, Americans would have to include our own Revolutionary colonists who defied King George, signed our Declaration of Independence, and fought our Revolutionary War using hit-and-run, ambush tactics (terrorism) instead of the "standard" way of fighting a war.

Yes, the world has become a more dangerous place since the demise of the Soviet Union in 1991.

Sectarian and ethnic rivalries and hatreds have sprung up in many corners of the world that were long suppressed and repressed during the cold war rivalry between the United States and the U.S.S.R.

Terrorism and its spread has become a legitimate focus of all countries, particularly in regard to terrorists acquiring weapons of mass destruction. Proliferation of nuclear weapons, particularly with regard to Iran and North Korea, has become a major focus in Western countries.

If one were to stand back, coldly and objectively, and view the world, terrorism (though terrible and often unpredictable) is not the menace that is capable of bringing about a world conflagration.

As horrific as it was, 9/11 was not the start of a new world war and, although a menace, cannot be equated with the likes of a Nazi Germany or even Imperial Japan after Pearl Harbor.

Terrorism and terrorists, despite the ranting of Osama bin Laden and his "death to America," are fundamentally incapable of world domination, and certainly not the menace the Bush administration has made them out to be.

Terrorism and terrorists should not be made into an enemy that can be confronted with large armies, or bombed into submission. Terrorists reside in the shadows, interspersed within the general population. They can, as was seen in the 9/11 atrocity, be capable of inflicting considerable havoc, death, and destruction. To anyone who lost loved ones in those attacks, 9/11 was and remains a terrible tragedy.

But, again, perspective must be maintained so terrorists' acts are not equated with menaces that require a full mobilization and sacrifice of the populace, as was done in the aftermath of the Japanese attack on Pearl Harbor. 9/11 was not the opening salvo to World War III, regardless of the Bush administration's ideas, ministrations, and declaration of its misnamed "War on Terror." The subsequent invasion of Afghanistan can be justified, but not Iraq.

The subsequent war in Iraq, by the invasion and conquering of a toothless foe, was not an imminent threat to the United States or the Persian Gulf (particularly after Iraq's defeat in the first Gulf War). The war in Iraq was a prime example of how not to confront terrorism and terrorists, and it was certainly not the way to project American military superiority. Large standing armies occupying countries with subjected peoples will not defeat terrorism. Instead, as now seen in Afghanistan, it can become a breeding ground that attracts more terrorists.

Pre-emptive invasions and occupations, even with good intentions, are destabilizing and unacceptable to the subjugated populations. This is neocolonialism, even if it is dressed up as freedom and democracy.

This is the lesson all empires eventually learned. The U.S. "empire" has refused to acknowledge and admit the futility of its present designs. Instead, it has embraced policies that exacerbate conflict, embolden terrorists, and promote terrorism, abandoning containment and stability as strategic American policy while making American "exceptionalism" a cause to bring American values, ideals, and beliefs to the rest of the world (even if it means at the point of a gun and in an "America knows what is best for you" attitude).

Communism, for all practical purposes, died with the demise of the Soviet Union.

China has become a primary manufacturer of many goods consumed in the United States while remaining Communist and adopting many capitalist measures and policies. It is hardly a monolith that threatens the world, despite its nuclear arsenal and authoritarian regime. It has become an economic colossus, not a military one.

Soviet Communism was shown to be a hollow reed that collapsed under its own contradictions and paradoxes, which ignored human nature and self-interest in its attempt to subordinate the individual to the collective interests of the state.

It was the "bogeyman" that scared the world for seventy-odd years and ended with a whimper. The free flow and exchange of ideas exposed its false premises, and it died relatively benignly.

Now, the world has a new "bogeyman"—terrorism and the misapplied "War on Terrorism"—and its face is Osama bin Laden.

When the Soviet Union died, America's cold war warriors needed a replacement, and Osama bin Laden and 9/11 terrorist attacks provided the perfect foil to initiate their "new" war against a new enemy to justify their need to fight evil and vanquish it totally and completely, in the words of George W. Bush, to "eliminate tyranny in the world" until all terrorists are vanquished from the Earth.

There may have been temporary economic dislocations and the legitimate desire to apprehend and punish the perpetrators of 9/11. The need to retaliate in Afghanistan was justified and supported by the world community.

Such sympathy was squandered in the misguided misadventure in Iraq.

Our insular conceit (that America knows what is good for other countries and, if necessary, America will thrust it upon them) is making for more instability in the world.

Could we help initiate World War III over terrorism? Is our fear so great that we lose all perspective on what terrorism is, what it is capable of, and what it can actually accomplish?

Irrational fear concocted by exaggerations and lies, formulated around the real horror of 9/11, is a way of distorting reality, making it appear real when, in fact, it is not. This is mendacity, cruel and misleading, perpetrated by those who see evil lurking everywhere, in some penultimate fight between good and evil. To George W. Bush, it was us (good) versus them (evil). Couple that with the fantasies of the neo-conservatives,[8] and you have the advent of a "War on Terrorism" juxtaposed with fundamentalist belief and flawed intellectual reasoning; a "witches brew" that helped bring about the worst foreign policy decisions ever made by this country.

---

8   *See the next chapter on neo-conservatism.*

NEO-CONSERVATISM

The following is a "Statement of Principles" formulated and stated on June 3, 1997, by the "Project for the New American Century." It represents the doctrine of the neo-conservatives.

It is reprinted here to show the essential ideology that was adopted by the Bush administration (particularly with many of its advocates holding *prominent* policy-making positions within the new Bush administration and in light of the subsequent events that were precipitated by and connected to the events of 9/11).

The world stands at its present precipice as a result.

June 3, 1997

American foreign and defense policy is adrift. Conservatives have criticized the incoherent policies of the Clinton administration. They have also resisted isolation impulses from within their own ranks. But conservatives have not confidently advanced a strategic vision of America's role in the world. They have not set forth guiding principles for American foreign policy. They have allowed differences over tactics to obscure potential agreement on strategic objectives. And they have not fought for a defense budget that would maintain American security and advance American interests in the new century.

We aim to change this. We aim to make the case and rally support for American global leadership.

As the twentieth century draws to a close, the United States stands as the world's preeminent power. Having led the West to victory in the Cold War, America faces opportunity and a challenge: Does the United States have the vision to build upon the achievements of past decades? Does the United States have the resolve to shape a new century favorable to American principles and interests?

We are in danger of squandering the opportunity and failing the challenge. We are living off the capital—both the military investments and the foreign policy achievements—built up by past administrations. Cuts in foreign affairs and defense spending, inattention to the tools of statecraft, and inconstant leadership are making it increasingly difficult to sustain American influence around the world. And the promise of short-term commercial benefits threatens to override strategic considerations. As a consequence, we are jeopardizing the nation's ability to meet present threats and to deal with potentially greater challenges that lie ahead.

We seem to have forgotten elements of the Reagan administration's success: a military that is strong and ready to meet both present and future challenges; a foreign policy that boldly and purposefully promotes American principles abroad; and national leadership that accepts the United States' global responsibilities.

Of course, the United States must be prudent in how it exercises its power. But we cannot safely avoid the responsibilities of global leadership or the costs that are associated with its exercise. America has a vital role in maintaining peace and security in Europe, Asia, and the Middle East. If we shirk our responsibilities, we invite challenges to our fundamental interests. The history of the twentieth century should have taught us that it is important to *shape circumstances before crises emerge,*[9] and to meet threats before they become dire. The history of this century should have taught us to embrace the cause of American leadership.

Our aim is to remind Americans of these lessons and to draw their consequences today. Here are four consequences: We need to increase defense spending significantly if we are to carry out our global responsibilities today and modernize our armed forces for the future. We need to strengthen our ties to democratic allies and

---

9   *This is the precursor to the Bush Doctrine of pre-emptive war. (Emphasis added.)*

to challenge regimes hostile to our interests and values.[10] We need to promote the cause of political and economic freedom abroad.

We need to accept responsibility for *America's unique role*[11] in preserving and extending an international order friendly to our security, our prosperity, and our principles.

Such a Reaganite policy of military strength and moral clarity may not be fashionable today. But it is necessary if the United States is to build on the successes of this past century and to ensure our security and our greatness in the next."[12]

Robert Merry, in his 2005 book, *Sands of Empire*, stated: "Neo-cons have embraced a Brave New World in which American exceptionalism holds sway everywhere and peoples around the globe abandon their own cultures in favor of Western ideals."

As for the neo-cons' "core philosophy," Merry wrote, "there really isn't one." They "make their way to whatever watering hole they can find."

Merry continued, "There is no distinctly neo-conservative bedrock of postulates or assumptions that provide a consistency of advocacy. Indeed, the underlying principles shift to fit the advocacy of the moment," with the last being "America must do everything possible on a global scale to ensure that its post cold war hegemony would continue throughout the world and into the future as far as the eye could see.

"And there we see the emergence of a foreign policy vision with no historical antecedents in the American experience. It is a vision of American world dominance perpetuated, maintained, and justified in the name of American ideals.… It is a temperament that favors pugnacity, bold thinking, and grand, encompassing visions of the world and the future, … a temperament that shows complexity, tactical adjustment, …

---

10 *This is American hubris and exceptionalism in the world. (Emphasis added.)*

11 *This is American hubris and exceptionalism in the world. (Emphasis added.)*

12 *Statement signers: Elliot Abrams, Gary Bauer, William J. Bennett, Jeb Bush, Dick Cheney, Eliot A. Cohen, Midge Decter, Paula Dobriansky, Steve Forbes, Aaron Friedberg, Francis Fukuyama, Frank Gaffney, Fred C. Ikle, Donald Kagan, Zalmay Khalilzad, I. Lewis Libby, Norman Podhoretz, Dan Quayle, Peter W. Rodman, Stephen P. Rosen, Henry S. Rowen, Donald Rumsfeld, Vin Weber, George Weigel, Paul Wolfowitz. (http://www.newamericancentury.org/statementofprinciples.htm)*

that could prove highly dangerous in a post cold war era characterized by brutal and persistent cultural and civilizational clashes. Those kinds of clashes can be adjudicated only with great difficulty, but they can be severely aggravated without much difficulty at all."

The neo-cons have all held sway in the Bush administration, which has been disastrous to America.[13] Its fantasy of regime change through pre-emptive invasion and occupation, its staunch support of Israel and the debasement of the Palestinians, its demonization of Iran and desire to overthrow the regime in Iran, and the condemnation of Russia (while ignoring Georgia's initiating the war in South Ossetia) created unnecessary instability in the world.

The neo-cons ignored history, disregarded ethnic and religious rivalry, had no respect for other cultures, and were the prime movers in pushing the expansion of U.S. hegemony that contributed to the growth of terrorism, particularly of the fundamentalist Islamic, Jihadist type.

This made the United States the primary initiator in fostering instability in the world.

The Bush administration derided the United Nations, scoffed at multilateral cooperation and diplomacy (unless it was dictated by the United States), and had no use for negotiating with adversaries without preconditions (which it alone determined), which the Bush administration considered "appeasement."[14]

With regard to present-day Russia, the Bush administration was arrogant with neo-con instigation. Viewing Russia as weak since the demise of the Soviet Union, the United States tried to take advantage by refusing to recognize Russia's fears (legitimate to them) of being encircled by American-backed clients (in Georgia; the Ukraine; the Baltic countries of Estonia, Latvia, and Lithuania; and the former Eastern bloc

---

13 *The McCain campaign for the presidency had neo-cons prominently in place as foreign policy advisors, with Senator Joe Lieberman (I.-Connecticut) as his leading neo-con advocate.*

14 *This is a distortion of what appeasement truly represents, which is giving away something without getting anything in return. Talking with an adversary (which we have traditionally done in previous administrations, e.g., Reagan with Gorbachev, Nixon with Mao is not appeasement.*

countries, in particular Poland, the Czech Republic, and Slovakia, while pushing for their inclusion in NATO), then advancing a missile defense system in Poland, saying it was for a future Iranian nuclear bomb threat (which Russia considers against them), and finally supporting Georgia with weaponry and military training and embracing Georgian President Saakashvili's brazen entry into South Ossetia (killing many civilians) while condemning Russia's counter move into Georgia.

The Bush administration refused to acknowledge the reality of spheres of influence (particularly *regional* spheres) of other great powers, believing that America, as the lone superpower, could muscle its way with impunity and press its vision, which precluded all other great powers from exercising their influence.

This is not to extol Russia for its overwhelming retaliatory response by invading Georgia, but we need to recognize we unnecessarily exacerbate world tensions by promoting and fostering strong military ties and pushing for NATO membership of countries that are right on Russia's doorstep.

As for the United States, it needs to step back from Bush's road to empire and imperialism that it was traveling.

The United States certainly does not want war with Russia. The Russian entry into Georgia should make us reconsider our own neocolonialism and overextended hegemony far from our own shores. Overheated oratory, opposed to the Russian invasion of Georgia, showed the reality of America's limitations.

A renewed cold war or, more incredibly, a war with Russia would be insane.

With the advent of the Bush administration and the events of 9/11, this country followed a neo-conservative path that intended to use our unmatched military supremacy to forge a new world dominated by the United States and intended to crush any opposition that stood to challenge this supremacy.

The Bush administration, unfortunately, did much damage in order to accomplish these ends. It mouthed such platitudes as acting as liberators to oppressed people, but was seen by those it "liberated" as aggressive invaders because the goal was not truly liberation, but domination and control.

To the American people, the Bush administration mouthed protection and security, but it wanted their compliance to its ambitions while demonizing all opposition as being against the national security of the United States.

September 11 was the catalyst (the event the Bush administration used) to connect, precipitate, and justify its pre-emptive wars.

The ambitions of the neo-conservatives were far outweighed by the realities of the world. Their fantasy of bringing democracy to the world's oppressed people (while dismissive of the tribal, ethnic, and religious fractures that permeate many of these lands, making them resistant to any form of government that does not resort to strong-arm tactics), is not possible. The end result was to make situations worse, more complicated, and to contribute to greater instability and increased terrorism.

Neo-conservative, self-righteous ideology produced Iraq, the worst foreign policy catastrophe since Vietnam. It antagonized allies, strained international cooperation, and declared pre-emptive war a national policy. It diminished our moral authority in the world and made America less safe, making every American a potential target by extremists bent on attacking America and anything American.

The Bush administration started the unnecessary war in Iraq under false pretences and shifting assumptions, and it was not forthright with the American people. It misused the American military as a tool to implement its ideology, rather than as a protector of the country.

The neo-con world view, until George W. Bush's arrival, had previously been dismissed as fringe thought and not consistent with the realities that existed in the world.

The neo-conservatives, though intelligent and articulate, have delusions of American grandeur. They represent the most dangerous destabilizing element in the world today.

Under Bush, American exceptionalism, which was once internal and isolationist and wary of outside entanglements (particularly wars in Europe), morphed into a desire to remake the world in its own image.

Since 9/11, America has become emboldened.

American "exceptionalism" has become twisted and entwined with hegemonic overreach, with its sphere of influence and footprint (military bases) worldwide, creating greater regional tensions that foment greater instability in the world.

America could have learned from Europe (with its colonialist past and having directly experienced the devastation of two world wars), but America was insulated from the devastation that Europe experienced in those world wars, along with the failures Europeans experienced with their own failed colonialism. Instead, our American exceptionalism of being a "chosen people" (and as a result of 9/11) contributed to the Bush administration unleashing some of its worst reactionary impulses.

Americans have to face the truth that the neo-cons, in their policies, and the Bush administration's hegemonic overreach, helped to create and expand the monster of Islamic terrorism.

IMPERIALISM, MILITARISM, FOREIGN POLICY, PRE-EMPTIVE WAR

American foreign policy is built on deception, just as its militarism justifies its bloated and unnecessary defense spending.

America is unchallenged militarily, and terrorism does not rise to the level of threat that justifies our defense expenditures.

With no real threat to justify America's present defense expenditures, it invents them, contrives an "axis of evil" whereby Iraq (now vanquished), Iran (surrounded, threatened, and demonized), and North Korea (now a nuclear power, since their demonization only accelerated their development of a nuclear device) were miraculously linked together as if to resemble the real Axis powers of World War II: vintage Nazi Germany, fascist Italy and Imperial Japan. The absurdity of the linkage of Iran and Iraq (they were antagonists in the Iraq and Iran War in the 1980s) and the paranoid, reclusive dictatorship of Kim's North Korea was lost on an administration that initiated the neo-conservative ideas of pre-emptive war, regime change, and democracy at the point of a gun.

American foreign policy has gone awry and lost its clarity.

According to the Associated Press, in a White House visit by Pakistan's new Prime Minister Galani, on July 28, 2008, President Bush said, twice, that he respects Pakistan's sovereignty. Just because he said it, does not mean he does it in reality. As the reality made clear, Bush authorized missiles to be fired into a Pakistani border village, supposedly going after a senior al Qaeda leader. Firing missiles into Pakistani territory, regardless of the evidence of known terrorists in a specific location, is an example of not respecting Pakistani sovereignty. Firing these missiles may have been done clandestinely or even in concurrence with the Pakistani government. However, overt admission of complicity would have jeopardized the Pakistani government, which officially rejects any intervention from any outside entity, including U.S. armed forces. Bush saying he respected another country's sovereignty, when in fact he did something that contradicts it, was an outright lie.

As is routine in the mainstream media, this latter fact was duly omitted. What was duly noted (in typical stenographic fashion by the media), is only what Bush said. That was it.

If you asked any American citizen, "Do you want to be lied to by your president?" I would venture to guess the answer would be a resounding, "No, absolutely not!"

It is the same with "appeasement," and the United States does not "torture." Bush said talking with an enemy is "appeasement." In reality, *appeasement* means giving something away and getting nothing in return. The United States gives away nothing by just talking. This is a deceptive misrepresentation of appeasement.

Saying the United States does not torture (when there is clear evidence that the United States does so) makes the credibility of the president all but zero. Approval ratings in the low 20s seem to confirm this. Yet it took the majority of Americans six years and two elections to finally come to the conclusion that they have been lied to by George W. Bush.

As for Iran, the Bush administration said it was committed to diplomacy. Then why do its actions clearly provoke that country?

Sending two aircraft carrier battle groups into the Persian Gulf was not a defensive action, as the administration asserted. Did the United States send such a lethal armada off Iran's coast and expect it to be seen as some sightseeing excursion? This was an openly provocative act.

Iran was already surrounded by enemies: Iraq and Turkey to the east, with Afghanistan and Pakistan to the west.

Iran's bombastic President Ahmadinejad (though not the Supreme Commander and final decision maker in Iran—the Ayatollah Khamenei has that role) is antagonistic in his own right, and is prone to provocative, irresponsible statements (denying the Holocaust, saying Israel should be wiped off the map), but for Iran to believe there is an imminent threat to its nation is not a far-fetched notion.

If the United States had such a similar hostile presence immediately off its shores, what would the United States do?

Duplicity and deception were not new inventions created by the Bush administration in its conduct of foreign policy.

However, with blatant consistency, the administration's pronouncements have been anything but truthful. In early 2007, the officially announced primary reason for the "surge" in Iraq was to give time for "political reconciliation" of the competing ethnic and religious factions of Shiites, Sunnis, and Kurds. It was never presented as a purely military increase to win the war.

Yet this was precisely what President Bush and Republican nominee John McCain presented to the American public. Overall violence in Iraq is down. Yet millions of Iraqis have been previously displaced from their homes. Prior to the surge, ethnic cleansing of Sunni neighborhoods led by Shiite militias occurred, resulting in Shia occupying many formerly Sunni homes. In Anbar Province, ethnic Sunnis (in previous alliance with al Qaeda terrorists fighting the American occupation) were appalled with al Qaeda terrorists' indiscriminate killing of Muslims in their suicide bombings and started going after these terrorists *in 2006, before* the surge began in the summer of 2007. The American forces, led by General Patreous, realized what was happening, co-opted the Anbar "awakening"[15] Sunni policy initiative (which was reducing the radical foreign Sunni terrorists' presence), and *portrayed* it as an American initiative. Meanwhile, Shiites, led by cleric Muqtada al-Sadr, decided to cease their intra-Shiite rivalry with its rival Shiite Badr Brigade, further reducing the overall violence.

---

15 *Sunni "awakening": These are former Iraqi Sunni insurgents, formed and led by local Sunni tribal chiefs (who were the main Sunni, Iraqi insurgency against the American presence in Iraq).*

Thus this country's overall decrease in violence was primarily due to Iraqi initiatives, not to the American "surge" strategy, yet this was and is presented as a purely American initiative, rather than Iraqi. Meanwhile, political reconciliation, the primary reason given for the "surge," was no closer to reality than before the "surge." And it was not mentioned, was not on the radar screen, when McCain said, "We are winning," and the "surge" was a success which contradicted the political reality.

As sanctioned by international law and the U.N. Charter, every country has the right to defend itself.

Prior to the attack on Pearl Harbor on December 7, 1941, it would have been totally within the United States' right to attack the Japanese armada before it struck. That was an imminent threat, and pre-emptive action would have been the appropriate action to take.

This has to be the standard to justify pre-emptive war. Further, America cannot use "Tonkin Gulf"[16] falsehoods as pretexts to justify war. When it does, America becomes no better than Hitler invading Poland in 1939 based on an imaginary threat, supposedly received by Germany, as to Poland's intentions to attack Germany. It is clear even Hitler realized he needed the cover of a "Polish threat" as justification for his attack.

In the context of the present day, Iraq and Saddam Hussein posed no imminent threat to the United States. The entire enterprise was a fabrication and exaggeration. Saddam had no weapons of mass destruction. It was a war of choice, setting in motion a sea change in our history. The United States made it clear that America no longer needed to abide by international law (not even a pretext to attack, or even a false pretence). The United States would wage war, and nothing or nobody could stop it.

---

16 *This was the basis for President Johnson asking the Congress for the Tonkin Gulf Resolution to legalize our escalation of the Vietnam War. There was no Tonkin Gulf attack, and clearly Johnson's intent was to escalate the war. So the attack was fabricated; therefore, the whole Vietnam escalation was based on a lie. To date there has been no official acknowledgment of this fact.*

It has been said that war is unpredictable. The Iraq War precipitated the move to Iraq of terrorists, and Iraq became the central front of Islamic militancy against the United States and the West.

The Iraqi insurgency and resistance against the U.S. invasion and occupation, unforeseen by the Bush administration, was a traditional reaction when one's country is invaded and occupied.

The Bush administration did not recognize the difference between an Iraqi insurgency that wanted U.S. troops out of Iraq and an enemy of al Qaeda-type Islamic terrorism, whose intention was to bring destabilization, destruction, and chaos.

It is only through the departure of the United States from Iraq that Iraq will be able to achieve a semblance of political reconciliation and some sort of political stabilization, which will not be achieved as long as the American military occupy the country.

In Vietnam, the American departure brought an end to that war. It didn't turn out the way the United States wanted, with a Communist government now throughout the country, but it did bring stability, no civil war ensued, and no dominoes fell in other countries. America learned to live with the result (50,000 American soldiers dead and the blow to the American ego notwithstanding).

Iraq requires an end to the U.S. presence.

There has been no enterprise that has so thoroughly transformed America from a nation that was revered and envied by so many in the world to one that is so despised by so many, so reviled that to be American is to be associated with torture, humiliation, and the killing of innocents, usually associated with the brutal and notorious regimes of the world (past and present).

Nicholas Kristof, writing an editorial in *The New York Times* on August 10, 2008, "Make Diplomacy, Not War," stated:

"Iraq and Afghanistan are the messes getting attention today, but they are only symptoms of a much broader cancer in American foreign policy.

"More than 1,000 American diplomatic positions are vacant because the Foreign Service is so short-staffed.... Some 1,100 could be hired for the cost of a single C-17 military cargo plane.

"In short, the United States is hugely overinvesting in military tools and under investing in diplomatic tools. The result is a lopsided foreign policy that antagonizes the rest of the world and is ineffective in tackling many modern problems."

Kristof quoted Defense Secretary Robert Gates, "The entire American diplomatic corps—about 6,500 people—is less than the staffing of a single aircraft carrier group.... The F-22 aircraft is produced by companies in 44 states; that's 88 senators.... China's rise is an excuse to grab tens of billions of dollars for the F-22, for an advanced destroyer, for new attack submarines."

Quoting Dennis Ross, a longtime Middle East peace negotiator: "Our intuitive approach to fighting terrorists and insurgents is to blow things up."

Kristof, summarizing a Rand Corporation report, added, "The Rand Corporation examined how 648 terror groups around the world ended between 1968 and 2006. It found that by far the most common way for them to disappear was to be absorbed by the political process. The second most common way was to be defeated by police work. In contrast, in only 7 percent of cases did military force destroy the terrorist group.

"There is no battlefield solution to terrorism," Kristof wrote that the report declared. "Military force usually has the opposite effect from what is intended."

As for our bloated defense budget, it is *unnecessary*, as there is no adversary capable of confronting the United States militarily. To have a defense budget larger than any since World War II is a ghastly abomination based on a distorted view of reality.

Our militarism, pre-emptive wars, and occupations of other countries need to be curtailed and tempered, returning to the containment and stability model, cooperation with allies in containing terrorism, and having direct and face-to-face diplomacy with adversaries.

As Churchill said, "It is better to jaw, jaw than war, war." The cold war is dead. Let's end the cold war mentality and see the world as it is. Ideology has no place in decisions of war and peace.

The idea of nation-building, through pre-emptive war and occupation, and transforming a failed state into a functioning, stable, democratic society, is a tantalizing notion that is unrealistic and needs to be discarded.

The main fallacy of this idea of nation-building is that it is brought to bear from the outside instead of evolving from within. It ignores the natural impulse that other cultures and their people resent imposition coming from without. They do not accept being told what is good for them. It doesn't matter if the ideas are based on sound reasoning or good intentions. It is overwhelmed by the fact that it is coming from outside the realm of the indigenous people themselves.

The idea of bringing freedom and democracy by invading a country should be seen as patently absurd. A stronger military will always defeat the weaker foe in traditional battlefield engagement. But as was seen in Vietnam, occupying a country and installing a government will always be seen as nothing more than a puppet regime and those who work with it, as collaborators.

Therefore, the Iraqi insurgency in the Iraq War against a foreign invasion and subsequent occupation was a natural consequence of resisting the invader.

Meanwhile, there is the question of Iran. Iran is not a threat. Iran is a proud country with a long history, a civilization that has existed for more than a millennium.

Iran invaded no country, and its last war was against Saddam Hussein's Iraq, which Saddam initiated in 1980 against Iran with the full backing of the United States (using military arms, intelligence, and chemical and biological weapons supplied by the United States).

Iran signed the Nuclear Nonproliferation Treaty, legally permitting it to develop nuclear power, which specifically disallows development of nuclear weapons. The U.S. *National Intelligence Estimate* report in December 2007 concluded Iran deliberately ceased any development of nuclear weapons capability in 2003.

So, why do we continue with the demonization of Iran? There is no doubt that Iran has a bombastic president who denies the Holocaust and wants the demise of Israel. On the last point, that would be the consensus of most Arab and Muslim countries, their people, and many Palestinians in the West Bank and Gaza. Modern-day Israel was resurrected in 1948 in what was then, and continues to be today, the heart of the Muslim world (as well as the heart of the religious tradition of the Jews and Christians). With their mixture of competing cultural and religious interests, conflict in this region is inevitable and continues unabated to this day.

Israel has become a modern, democratic state despite the hatred and animosity that surrounds it. Though not acknowledged, Israel has nuclear weapons, a fact known throughout the world, and that, of course, includes Iran.

Since Israel's 1967 war against Egypt and Syria, and the success of that war, Israel became an occupying power. With its victory, Israel annexed the Golan Heights (Syria), the West Bank (Jordan), and the Gaza Strip (until Israel's 2005 unilateral withdrawal), and expanded the settlement of Jews in those areas. It annexed Jerusalem and made Jerusalem its capital. Along with the expulsion of Palestinians[17] in the formation of modern day Israel in 1948 (from Palestinian territory that was part of Jordan from which Israel was created), there remains these festering issues that divide the conflicting sides, issues that are unresolved and have been intractable, considering the extreme antipathy of both sides.

That Iran sides with its Muslim brothers (though it is predominately Shiite while most Palestinians are Sunni) opposing

---

17 *This has resulted in the key Palestinian issue, "the right of return" of Palestinians that were forcibly removed to make way for the modern re-establishment of Israel in 1948.*

Israel should not be hard to fathom, along with the United States as the main benefactor of Israel and America's own tortured history and relations with Iran.[18]

The Bush administration's pre-emptive war against Saddam Hussein's Iraq (with a Shiite majority) effectively established Shiite dominance in Iraq with Saddam's removal (thereby unwittingly establishing a natural ally with Shiite Iran). With terrorism so dominant on America's mind, the United States seems a country almost unbalanced, pursuing quixotic policies, and most profoundly, without provocation, made Iran a part of the "axis of evil."

The United States has lost its sense of "clarity."

In a person, such behavior might be considered delusional. When it exists in the lone superpower left in the world, this is dangerous, not only to itself, but to the rest of the world.

As for negotiations with adversaries (a long-standing policy of the United States), if America is to accept the idea of negotiations literally, negotiations must be without any preconditions. It is not negotiation when one side is presented with preconditions that must be met before the other will sit down and negotiate. With preconditions, it becomes an ultimatum, by the stronger side toward the weaker side. In essence, "surrender first and then we will consider meeting with you."

True negotiation is a meeting by competing sides with no preconditions.

As for the idea of "appeasement," that means to cede away something during negotiation and get nothing in return (as in Prime Minister Chamberlain of Britain ceding away part of Czechoslovakia to Germany's Hitler in 1937 without getting anything in return from Hitler. This has been the classic example of "appeasement" since that time). It is not "appeasement" just to sit down with another side without preconditions.

18 The CIA instigated the overthrow of the legitimately elected government in Iran in 1953 and the establishment of the brutal Shah regime in Iran who became an American ally we supplied with U.S. arms [planes, tanks, and artillery]. Later with the Iranian takeover of the U.S. Embassy in Tehran in 1979, and the subsequent Iranian Revolution that established the sectarian rule of IAtollah Khoumani, there is reason to understand the current antipathy that exists between the U.S. and Iran.

This has been the ploy of the Bush administration with regard to Iran. The Bush administration refused to negotiate without preconditions with Iran, saying to do so would be "appeasement." As "appeasement" is viewed as weakness, its use by the Bush administration with regard to Iran was clearly deceiving, a way of taking something positive (diplomatic negotiations) and misrepresenting it (appeasement). This is a propagandist method usually associated with dictatorial regimes.

In the case with Iran, the United States wanted Iran to literally commit "appeasement," to cede its nuclear program before the United States would consider any negotiations. Iran refused to concede anything, deflecting attention to its nuclear activities, saying it was acting legally as a member of the Nuclear Nonproliferation Treaty, whereby it agreed to preclude any desire to produce nuclear weapons, but it is permitted to develop nuclear power for nonmilitary means.

The Bush administration further demonized Iran, saying Iran supports terrorists and terrorism, yet it was America that pre-emptively invaded two countries. As indicated previously, America has the largest nuclear arsenal in the world; America surrounds Iran with allies (Turkey and Pakistan, as well as occupied Iraq and Afghanistan) and two aircraft carrier groups actively patrolling in the Persian Gulf, directly off the coast of Iran, and Israel has nuclear weapons, while Iran has none. Iran only has missiles that can reach Israel with conventional warheads. To say a non-nuclear weapons power is an imminent threat to the preeminent nuclear weapons power is absurd; yet it is Iran that is presented as the threat!

This so-called "logic" of Iran as a threat was apparently believed by the majority of the American people as indicated in the polls—a clear example of the effective use of administration propaganda, masked as the truth and foisted on the American people, which is ably stenographed and enabled by the mainstream media without any contrary opinions to challenge this propaganda and trumpeted by active military generals serving improperly as political tools of the Bush administration.

David Barstow, writing in *The New York Times*,[19] revealed how the public was duped by "military analysts" who were retired military officers

---

19   David Barstow, *"Pentagon Suspends Briefings for Analysts,"* New York Times, April 26, 2008.

connected "to military contractors vested in the very war policies they were asked to assess on air." As Barstow stated, "Those business relationships are hardly ever disclosed to the viewers.… Internal Pentagon … documents reveal … a symbiotic relationship in which the usual dividing lines between government and journalism have been obliterated." The Pentagon described the analysts "as message force multipliers" or "surrogates" who could be counted on to deliver administration "themes and messages" to millions of Americans, "in the form of their own opinions.… A few expressed regret for participating in what they regarded as an effort to dupe the American public with propaganda dressed as independent military analysis."

As Americans, we must ask certain questions.

Again, if there are no real threats, imminent or otherwise, to the military superiority of the United States, why does the United States act as if it is vulnerable?

Why should we believe these regimes have a death wish of assured annihilation if they were to launch a nuclear attack on the United States or its allies? Even though Iran is years away from developing a nuclear device, the United States acts as though Iran is intent on using these weapons once it has them in place.

Why is there no acknowledgment that no nuclear power has ever used a nuclear bomb since the United States bombed Hiroshima and Nagasaki

With no real threats, why do we continue to pursue policies as if these threats exist?

Is it just to fuel the defense industry, to maintain it and keep it profitable?

Why are we developing an anti-missile defense system that doesn't work and is unnecessary? (In August 2008, Bush signed an agreement with Poland to install such a system when it becomes operational.)

According to Robert Scheer,[20] in a June 3, 2008, *Baltimore Sun* article entitled, "Wasteful Weapons," the United States is spending trillions on

20 *Robert Scheer, The Pornography of Power, Twelve, Hachette Book Group, USA 2008.*

obsolete defense systems. Scheer stated, "Isn't it bizarre that the biggest peacetime military budget in U.S. history … is not even discussed in the current presidential contest…. Defense spending has become enshrined in our political system as a totem rather than a policy program to be critically examined."

Exposing 9/11 as the catalyst, Scheer described "a madcap spending spree on wars and weapons having little, if anything, to do with fighting terrorism … and everything to do with sustaining an enormously bloated defense industry threatened with extinction because of the demise of the Communist enemy."

As an example, the Virginia class submarine costs $2.5 billion each; they are produced in Connecticut, home state of Senator Joe Lieberman, (I.); according to Lieberman, "If we do not move to produce two submarines a year as soon as possible, we are in serious danger of falling behind." Behind who? These submarines were designed for battle in deep oceans, and the enemy these ships were designed for ceased to exist twenty years ago. Terrorists do not have canoes, much less submarines operating in deep oceans.

To repeat, the age of world war, imperialism, and conquest ended some sixty-five years ago with the defeat of Nazi Germany and Imperial Japan, and the dawn of the nuclear age. An age of nuclear standoff and cold war between the United States and the Soviet Union ended abruptly with the demise of the latter in 1991.

The world has entered into a new age, unleashing conflicts and turmoil of long-simmering ethnic and religious hatreds and political oppression that were previously held in check and repressed by the two main antagonists, the United States and the U.S.S.R., with the hegemony and influence they each exerted.

However, these new types of conflicts—the dissolution of Yugoslavia, the Taliban in Afghanistan, genocide in Rwanda and presently in Sudan, and even the U.S.-instigated war in Iraq—do not rise to the level of conflicts that can remotely be conceived as threatening a world war.

With regard to Iran, the United States is unable to state our problems based on all the facts and the reality as it truly exists.

Iran presents a complicated picture that cannot be summarized by sound bite snippets taken out of context and presented as something that reflects anything closely resembling reality.

Iran's leadership structure is complicated and misunderstood. Despite President Ahmadinejad's rhetoric, he does not represent or have the final authority in Iran's leadership hierarchy. That rests with the mullahs, the religious ayatollahs, headed by Ayatollah Khamenei. The mullahs have the ultimate say on policy in Iran. They may be ultraconservative and, in terms of Western values, repressive of the people. They are, however, not insane or suicidal, and they would not risk the certain annihilation of Iran.

Worse, more terrible dictatorships, armed with nuclear weapons, have existed (the Soviet Union) and they were deterred successfully through direct contact, negotiation, and diplomacy. They were not "appeased," the latest misused and misunderstood policy of the Bush administration, and they were contained successfully.

Why is it so hard to contemplate successfully containing Iran, even with nuclear weapons?

With the massive U.S. footprint in the Muslim countries, it is clear the United States represents the greatest threat to further instability in the Middle East, not Iran.

The Bush presidency has been a rogue administration with an odd mixture of fundamentalist visions of Armageddon juxtaposed against the neo-conservative delusion of democracy through pre-emptive war. It supports Israel as the beleaguered victim that needs to be protected at all costs, belying the reality of Israel being a nuclear power that subjugates the Palestinian people in the occupied territories.

Early on, since its inception in 1948, there was understanding and even compassion for Israel's plight, surrounded as it was by hostile Arab neighbors.

Yet, much has changed since that war. Over forty years, Israel has exacerbated the conflict by making Jerusalem its capital, permitting the installation of settlements on Palestinian lands in the West Bank (and

Gaza until its unilateral withdrawal in 2005), while building a twenty-two-foot concrete wall around the West Bank, essentially sealing off the Palestinians from Israel proper.

Much of the terrorism against the Israelis is instigated by Israel's brutalizing and marginalizing of the Palestinians, allowing the settlement expansion in the West Bank by settlers expropriating Palestinians from where they live, while erecting a series of checkpoints that further restrict Palestinian movement.

Anyone critical of Israeli policies is immediately branded and condemned as anti-Semitic, thus precluding any dialogue. In the United States, and particularly in the Congress, there is almost complete knee-jerk support for Israel. The media is totally uncritical of, supportive of, and biased toward Israel.

Israel has become almost a third-rail issue in the United States, untouchable and sacrosanct. There is no discussion of Israel's policies.

Fundamentalist Christians support Israel unequivocally, aligned with Israel as the epicenter of their apocryphal beliefs in a second coming of Christ.

AIPAC, the well-heeled organization of neo-conservative Jews whose lobbying and indirect political funding of candidates and sitting Congressmen is almost universal, exercises outsized influence in all matters concerning Israel. Its activities essentially suppress any discussion of any consequence, if any criticism of Israel is suspected.

The Holocaust is, of course, the unmentionable event whose memory is seared (as it should be) in the minds of most people, which insulates Israel from any criticism, particularly in the United States.

But Americans must go beyond heartfelt sympathy and empathy for Israel and the Jewish people and begin to be fair-minded with regard to the Palestinians. Extolling Israel's side (despite whatever Israel does), while demonizing the Palestinian side as illegitimate and labeled as terrorists, only exacerbates the situation. No political solution is possible under the present circumstances without the United States acting as a truly neutral mediator and facilitator between the Israelis and the

Palestinians. President Carter came closest in 1979 when helping President Anwar Sadat and Prime Minister Menachem Begin broker Egypt's peace with Israel. All other efforts since then have failed.

As for Saddam Hussein, he would never have shared weapons of mass destruction with terrorists such as Osama bin Laden, as these terrorists were a direct threat to him and his regime. The idea, perpetrated by the Bush administration, that Saddam would pass weapons of mass destruction on to terrorists that would ensure his own demise, as well as Iraq's, was utter nonsense.

No country possessing such weapons has actually used them. Britain, France, India, Pakistan, China, Israel, and now North Korea have never attacked another nuclear power.

Their only use has been confined to the United States using them to end World War II against an enemy (Japan) that did not possess them.

To be sure, threats have been issued from one to the other, but actual use has not happened. The devastation and potential for total annihilation is and has been the rationale against their use.

It is not lost on the "rogue" regimes of Iran and North Korea that having such weapons constitutes a sort of inviolable guarantee that they will not be attacked by another nuclear weapons power.

The Bush administration used terms such as "blackmail" in its reference to these regimes, prompting its declaration of its right to pre-emptively attack whenever and wherever a "potential" threat is evidenced if a regime is proceeding to acquire nuclear weapons.

Yet, it is only the United States that appears ready to consider developing and using tactical nuclear weapons in conventional wars. This would constitute the most dangerous shift in the world (if nuclear tactical weapons were to be used in conventional conflicts).

Thus, it appears there is one unmistakable conclusion to be made: The United States, with a policy of pre-emptive war, constitutes the primary destabilizing force in the world.

It is madness to equate terrorism as an existential threat to all humanity. Dictators and dictatorships have always existed. Though democracy, in its many forms, constitutes a preferred type of rule by most people, the fact that authoritarian rule, in and of itself, is an imminent threat to democratic states does not conform to reality. It may be a humanitarian disaster to the people of North Korea to have to endure the regime of Kim, but North Korea with Kim does not present an imminent threat to the world, even with nuclear weapons.

What nuclear weapons have done is to make nuclear war unthinkable. That is the only sane reality. Threatening their use is madness. Nonproliferation should be pursued simply because the more regimes that have them, the greater the chance of accidents (as well as the possibility of terrorists stealing some unsecured nuclear device), not their deliberate use.

Mature diplomacy, which is not appeasement, must be the way of the world. Saber-rattling, pre-emptive wars against petty dictatorships ratchet up the unpredictable consequences of war and misdirect the urgent need to prevent terrorists from acquiring a nuclear device.

There is no doubt that the world would be safer without any weapons of mass destruction, particularly nuclear weapons. However, this is not a realistic proposition. Countries have them and retain them because they are the ultimate deterrent against an attack.

Stalin, perhaps the most brutal man to walk the Earth, had such weapons and never resorted to their use because in doing so he, the U.S.S.R., and the world would not have survived. The deterrence factor of "mutually assured destruction" worked perfectly. It has thus worked with Pakistan and India (though both have had conventional wars, primarily over Kashmir); neither seriously contemplated the use of nuclear weapons, knowing full well the consequences of such use would be their own demise.

Israel exists among hostile neighbors primarily because of their own nuclear weapons, with all their adversaries knowing full well the consequences of a nuclear attack would be their own demise.

China has the world's third largest arsenal, has the means of delivery, but does not brandish this hardware. By the world's economic engagement with this giant, there is no serious contemplation of China's use of these weapons. China may exploit its people and is a dictatorship using capitalistic economic principles, but it is has become a member of the world community even without being a Western-type democracy.

Russia has inherited these weapons from the demise of the U.S.S.R. Though far from being a free and open society, it is no threat to the world community (despite its retaliatory war with Georgia).

It is only the United States that overreacts to the idea of threats coming from countries that either just acquired or may get these weapons, namely, North Korea and Iran.

China, Russia, Japan, and South Korea may mouth their displeasure with North Korea and its development of nuclear weapons, but they are hardly overexercised with this "threat." South Korea, supposedly the most threatened, continues to call for continued engagement with the North as the best way of dealing with it.

If stateless terrorists pose a threat to the world, it is with the possibility of them acquiring some sort of nuclear device (such as a "dirty bomb" of spent nuclear materials). Thus there is an urgent need to secure all nuclear materials by all states with nuclear facilities. It would be suicidal for any regime to knowingly pass nuclear weapons to terrorists.

All dictators secure power, do everything in their power to maintain it and retain it, but they are containable. Their desire is to continue to rule. They are anything but suicidal, unless they were threatened with their own extinction. They are predictable in this way.

When the United States can obliterate any state five times over, what state poses any real threat?

Ted Galen Carpenter, vice president for defense and foreign policy studies at the Cato Institute, has stated, "The North Korean regime … has never shown signs of suicidal behavior. And attacking the United States would definitely be suicidal."

As Carpenter indicated, "We have deterred other strange and ruthless regimes in the past, most notably the Soviet Union under Josef Stalin and China under Mao Tse-Tung."

Reality and diplomacy have to be the proper rationale for dealing with North Korea and Iran. Unnecessary bluster, threats, and intimidation, as well as any proposals for pre-emptive action, are unnecessarily risky behaviors that were never seriously contemplated against the real adversaries aforementioned.

Kim Jong-il wants what all dictators want: to retain power and control over his country and its people. Kim has neither the wherewithal nor the power to expand that domain beyond North Korea.

The United States needs to be the supreme diplomat in the world with the demeanor of an experienced, wise diplomat fully engaged in the world and respectful of others with different values and ethnic and religious backgrounds. America needs to resume its place in the world community of nations, committed to the peaceful resolution of disputes in the world.

America's actions seem more like a person cornered in a room by thugs, rather than a calm, collected contributor of wisdom and experience, dealing with an unruly teenager venturing for independence.

The United States often acts as if it is superior in the world, a "chosen people" that should be immune from the world's strife. That it is "the American way, or the highway" leads many others in the world to view the United States with contempt, suspicion, and fear.

If the United States were to concede it is an integral part of the world community of people, America could defuse much of the deep-seated hatred it now engenders in the world.

It is America's humanity, its generous, informal, relaxed nature as people, that needs to be its face in the world.

To be sure, the threat of terrorists gaining the possession of a nuclear device constitutes a threat to the world.

What all the world's nuclear powers must guard against is the acquisition of these weapons by terrorists.

But the idea of any regime possessing these weapons and somehow passing them on to terrorists is unthinkable. It appears again the United States is the only country consumed with the idea that such an occurrence is fathomable, and therefore drumbeats for wars of pre-emption. It seems the United States is the only country willing to risk all to prevent the proliferation of these weapons.

The United States must stop attempting to remake the world in its own likeness. It is not possible and is futile. If America were to adopt a strategy of mutual respect toward other countries, and stop conjuring enemies that cannot plausibly be any real threat to it, through diplomacy and engagement, the United States and the rest of the world can manage, contain, and deter whatever conflicts threaten national and international stability. By mutual association, coalitions, and cooperation, the world can effectively pursue and contain terrorist networks and bring them to justice.

U.S. policies are and have been a primary factor in bringing about much of the terrorism in the world today.

Since the United States is the main destabilizing force in the world, until it retreats from its occupation of Islamic countries, and ends its support of the oppressive regimes in these Muslim countries, America will only exacerbate the terrorism against the United States.

America must return as a fair arbiter and an objective broker between Israel and the Palestinians and refrain from knee-jerk support of Israel. The United States must insist Israel withdraw from the occupied territories and dismantle all of the settlements in those territories as the basis for America's aid to Israel.

America must accept its culture as unique only to itself and embrace mutual respect, tolerance, and engaged diplomacy and stability as the primary goals of U.S. foreign policy.

The mission of the U.S. military must return to defense of the country, rejecting a policy of pre-emptive war against countries that pose no imminent threat to America.

WAR IN IRAQ

President Bush, on August 11, 2008, responding to the Russian invasion of neighboring "sovereign" Georgia, said, "Such an action is unacceptable in the twenty-first century."

Bush obviously had no such qualms when he invaded a "sovereign" Iraq in March 2003.

Sovereignty, as defined by *Webster's*, is the ultimate, supreme power in a state.

A pre-emptive invasion against a sovereign nation is an act of aggression and a direct violation against the very idea of sovereignty. There is no room to spin sovereignty. The invasion of Iraq was a direct violation of its sovereignty.

Six years and running, what more can be said and written about the Iraq misadventure? It was a war of choice and unnecessary. As addressed in the previous chapter, Saddam's Iraq posed no imminent threat to the United States or anyone else. Saddam had no connection to terrorists, Osama bin Laden, and al Qaeda. Saddam had no connection to 9/11, and Saddam did not possess weapons of mass destruction. These were a contrived bill of goods, a subterfuge, a false excuse to go to war.

By the time of the 2006 Congressional elections, the people had concluded the war was wrong, and the return of Democratic majorities in the House and Senate[21] were, in effect, a direct rebuke of Bush and his war.

---

21 *Though attaining majorities was not enough to bring an end to the war.*

Though the war continues, with its end (presumably) to occur with the new Obama administration, it is instructive to recall some of the various terms of demonology and deception that Americans have been subjected to since January 2002, when Bush, in his State of the Union speech, made Iraq part of the "axis of the evil," which was to be the opening salvo that laid the groundwork for his eventual invasion of Iraq.

The Center of Public Integrity has a data base of 935 *false statements* regarding Iraq prior to the invasion in March 2003, starting as early as October 11, 2001, exactly one month after the 9/11 attacks by al Qaeda.

Here is a partial listing:

October 11, 2001. President Bush: "We know [Saddam Hussein has] been developing weapons of mass destruction."

January 29, 2002. President Bush: "States like these and their terrorist allies constitute an axis of evil arming to threaten the peace of the world; by seeking weapons of mass destruction, these regimes pose a grave and growing danger; they could provide these arms to terrorists."

February 3, 2002. Secretary of State Colin Powell: "We suspect they are developing weapons of mass destruction. We more than suspect it, we know it."

February 11, 2002. President Bush: "And this president is not going to allow regimes such as Iran, Iraq, and North Korea to threaten our way of life."

February 24, 2002. Secretary of Defense Donald Rumsfeld: "They have advanced their weapons of mass destruction programs."

March 13, 2002. President Bush: "[Iraq is] a nation which has weapons of mass destruction and apparently is not afraid to use them."

March 18, 2002. President Bush: "We will not allow one of the world's most dangerous leaders to have the world's most dangerous weapons, and hold the United States and our friends and allies hostage."

March 22, 2002. President Bush: "He is a dangerous man who possesses the world's most dangerous weapons."

March 24, 2002. Vice President Dick Cheney: "In the case of Saddam Hussein, we have a dictator who is clearly pursuing these deadly weapon capabilities."

June 10, 2002. Secretary of Defense Rumsfeld, when asked about the statement made by the Iraqi government the previous day that Iraq had no weapons of mass destruction and was not developing any, replied: "They are lying. Next."

August 26, 2002. Vice President Cheney: "Simply stated, there is no doubt that Saddam Hussein now has weapons of mass destruction. There is no doubt he is amassing them to use against our friends, against our allies, and against us."

September 4, 2002. Secretary of State Powell: "It is absolutely a fact that Iraq has not complied with these resolutions to get rid of weapons of mass destruction."

September 8, 2002. Vice President Cheney: "But we know with absolute certainty that he is using his procurement system to acquire the equipment he needs in order to enrich uranium to build a nuclear weapon."

September 14, 2002. President Bush: "Today Saddam Hussein has the scientists and the infrastructure for a nuclear weapon. Should his regime acquire fissile material, it would be able to build a nuclear weapon within a year.... By supporting terrorists groups ... Saddam Hussein's regime has proven itself a grave and gathering danger."

September 15, 2002. National Security Advisor Condoleezza Rice: "Well, there are clearly links between Iraq and terrorism and there are al Qaeda personnel that have been spotted in Baghdad. There is some evidence that there have been various meetings concerning Iraqi personnel and al Qaeda personnel."

September 18, 2002. President Bush: "And he's developing weapons of mass destruction. We must deal with him."

September 18, 2002. White House Press Secretary Ari Fleischer: "Iraq's basic position is to say that it has no weapons of mass destruction. That is a black lie."

September 20, 2002. Deputy Defense Secretary Paul Wolfowitz: "We've got to make it clear that support for terrorism in an age of weapons of mass destruction is simply not something that any country can be in the business of, and that's the heart of the issue with Iraq."

September 26, 2002. White House Press Secretary Fleischer: "These are links between al Qaeda and Baghdad."

September 28, 2002. President Bush: "The Iraqi regime possesses biological and chemical weapons.... The regime has long-standing and continuing ties to terrorist groups, and there are al Qaeda terrorists inside Iraq. This regime is seeking a nuclear bomb, and with fissile material could build one in a year."

September 28, 2002. President Bush: "[Saddam is] a man who loves to link up with al Qaeda.... Saddam Hussein has got a choice, and that is, he can disarm."

October 1, 2002. President Bush: "But disarming this man is necessary, because he faces a true threat to the United States."

October 2, 2002. President Bush: "We know the designs of the Iraqi regime. In defiance of pledges to the U.N., it has stockpiled biological and chemical weapons.... Military option is my last choice."

October 2, 2002. Vice President Cheney: "We've already found confirmation that the al Qaeda terrorists are pursuing weapons of mass destruction. At the same time there's a danger of terror groups joining together with the regimes that have or are seeking to build such weapons. In Iraq, we know Saddam Hussein is pressing forward with these capabilities."

October 4, 2002. President Bush: "This is a man who said he wouldn't have weapons of mass destruction. Yet he does."

October 7, 2002. President Bush: "We know that Iraq and the al Qaeda terrorist network share a common enemy: the United States of

America. We know that Iraq and al Qaeda have had high-level contacts that go back a decade.... The evidence indicates that Iraq is reconstituting its nuclear weapons program."

October 8, 2002. President Bush: "But if [the U.N. is] unable to act, and if Saddam Hussein can't do what he said he would do, which is to disarm, this country will lead a coalition and disarm him, for the sake of peace."

October 14, 2002. President Bush, as he signs the Iraq Resolution: "The Iraqi regime is a serious and growing threat to peace. On the commands of a dictator, the regime is armed with biological and chemical weapons, possesses ballistic missiles, promotes international terror, and seeks nuclear weapons. And Iraq's combination of weapons of mass destruction and ties to terrorist groups and ballistic missiles would threaten the peace and security of many nations."

November 4, 2002. President Bush: "This is a man who has had al Qaeda connections.... He is a threat.... Imagine this guy having a nuclear weapon. Imagine what it would mean to America and our friends."

December 7, 2002. Secretary of Defense Rumsfeld: "The United States knows that Iraq has weapons of mass destruction."

January 10, 2003. Vice President Cheney: "That is why confronting the threat posed by Iraq is not a distraction from the War on Terror. It is absolutely crucial to winning the War on Terror."

January 20, 2003. President Bush: "He's not disarming."

January 22, 2003. President Bush: "My hope is that Saddam Hussein will disarm voluntarily, that's my hope. I take seriously the commitment of any troops in combat. I desire peace."

January 27, 2003. White House Press Secretary Fleischer: "This is about peace, and this is about protecting people in the region and the American people from Saddam Hussein, who has weapons that kill millions."

January 31, 2003. Vice President Cheney: "Saddam Hussein's pursuit of weapons of mass destruction poses grave danger—not only to his neighbors, but also to the United States. His regime aids and protects terrorists, including members of al Qaeda."

February 3, 2003. Secretary of State Powell, in his address to the U.N.: "But what I want to bring to your attention today is the potentially more sinister nexus [between Iraq and the al Qaeda terrorist network]."

February 6, 2003. President Bush: "The Secretary of State [Colin Powell] has now briefed the United Nations Security Council on Iraq's illegal weapons programs, its attempts to hide those weapons, and its links to terrorist groups. I want to thank Secretary Powell for his careful and powerful presentation of the facts.... Iraq has sent bomb-making and document forgery experts to work with al Qaeda. Iraq has provided al Qaeda with weapons and chemical and biological weapons training."

February 6, 2003. Secretary of Defense Rumsfeld, referring to Colin Powell's speech at the U.N.: "He gave a fine presentation. He laid out the facts. It is clear the Iraqis have weapons of mass destruction."

February 6, 2003. Deputy Defense Secretary Wolfowitz: "I think Secretary Powell made a powerful case of how containment wasn't working, that he is continuing to develop his weapons.... It is very clear that Iraq is part of the war on terrorism; that we are dealing with terrorist networks that are connected in part to Baghdad."

February 8, 2003. Secretary of Defense Rumsfeld, regarding Powell's speech to the U.N. Security Council: "He presented not opinion, not conjecture, but facts demonstrating Iraq's ongoing pursuit of nuclear, chemical, and biological weapons; and its ties to terrorists networks including al Qaeda.... It is difficult to believe there still could be a question in the minds of reasonable people open to the facts before them. The threat is there to see."

February 11, 2003. White House Press Secretary Fleischer: "I think when Secretary Powell went to New York and talked about the evidence we have of the ties between Iraq and al Qaeda, he did so on the basis of knowledge, on the basis of fact."

February 20, 2003. President Bush: "Saddam Hussein will be disarmed one way or the other."

March 4, 2003. White House Press Secretary Fleischer: "The president does believe that Iraq is a direct threat to the United States as a result of Iraq having weapons of mass destruction, particularly biological and chemical weapons."

March 16, 2003. Vice President Cheney: "And we believe he has, in fact, reconstituted nuclear weapons."

March 19, 2003. President Bush, as the invasion of Iraq began: "Our nation enters this conflict reluctantly—yet our purpose is sure. The people of the United States and our friends and allies will not live at the mercy of an outlaw regime that threatens the peace with weapons of mass destruction."

Invading Iraq and having no plan on how to stabilize the country (after pre-emptively invading it) is the height of incompetence, and it captures the real essence of the Bush administration. (It was duplicated in its response to Hurricane Katrina.)

The whole Iraq War misadventure, particularly the way the Bush administration presented it, is emblematic of the deceptive propaganda being perpetrated on the people of this country.

The need to resort to these unsavory methods was a dead giveaway to the contrived nature of the entire enterprise. It so disrespected the American people that the truth had to be hidden lest the entire unholy exercise would be exposed for the sham it was. That it was done so blatantly is astonishing.

What has been perpetrated on the American people is a clear case of exaggeration and deception. Arthur Schlesinger, Jr., historian and advisor to President Kennedy, described it succinctly in *The Washington Post* on June 28, 2003, in his article, "The Imperial Presidency Redux": "The weapons of mass destruction—where are they? Many Americans do not like to be manipulated and deceived."

This represents, in unmistakably clear language, what it is Americans have been subjected to, and it is emblematic of the premise set forth within these pages.

As we have been witnesses, John McCain continually credits the "surge" as the reason for the decline in violence in Iraq.

Richard Appel, Jr., writing in *The New York Times* on August 22, 2008, said, "Although the 'surge' is often described as the turning point that led to lower violence, a number of American officers contend the awakening, that began well before the surge in 2006 in Anbar Province and continued in Baghdad last year, was the most significant reason for the decline. In some places, American casualties plunged within weeks of the Sunnis joining with American forces."

The deception continued.

MAINSTREAM MEDIA

Jefferson said, "An informed citizenry is the best defense against tyranny by the State."

When Edward R. Murrow was the executive editor of the CBS series *See It Now* in the early 1950s and Senator Joe McCarthy (R.-Wisconsin) made exaggerated and unfounded claims of so many "Communists in the State Department," Murrow did not hesitate to challenge him, at great risk to himself and CBS's reputation, considering the fear of Communists and Communism that prevailed during those times.

During the Bush administration, with terrorism replacing Communism as the chief threat (both real and imagined), where was the mainstream media during the run-up to the Iraq War, when weapons of mass destruction, "mushroom clouds," and Saddam in league with al Qaeda were being foisted upon the American people in the aftermath of the 9/11 terrorist attacks? The mainstream media was certainly not challenging those claims. It dutifully reported (as stenography) those claims as fact, hardly fulfilling its role as skeptic and objective reporter of the "news" to keep the public informed. Ditto for the overwhelming majority of the "people's" representatives in both houses of Congress, except for the likes of Senators Byrd, Feingold, Kennedy, and a few others (none of whom commanded the widespread respect and following that Murrow did) who were roundly criticized and condemned as soft on terrorism and unpatriotic, almost considered un-American in their dissenting views.

All the mainstream media was derelict in its duty to uncover the exaggerations of WMDs in Iraq that were promoted by the Bush administration.

It did not challenge the conventional wisdom until it became so blatantly obvious it could not be denied any longer. If reporters had searched the Internet, they would have found sufficient grounds to unearth the truth (or at least question the administration's claims). Instead, we got a regurgitation of whatever the White House was promoting.

The mainstream media gave a pass to the White House in fear of retribution (denial of access) by the administration if it were not on board with the need to go to war.

To what extent ownership of the mainstream media by big corporate owners inhibited its coverage or inhibited its criticism is not a firmly established fact; certainly, there have been no admissions by present or former media executives.

Keith Olberman of MSMBC has been, at least since 2005, one of the few administration critics in the mainstream media who has pointed out that Bush and his administration's policies have been wrongheaded, incompetent, and ridden with war profiteering and cronyism; their disregard for the rule of law breath-taking, and their ideological bent and neo-conservative influence disastrous over both terms of the Bush presidency. Olberman comes closest to revealing this truth, but again, Bush bashing had become easier, even viewer friendly, as polls showed Bush's popularity had dropped precipitously after Katrina, and the war was seen as a mistake. The media had abandoned its obligation to keep the people informed; the people were certainly not served credibly by the mainstream media early in the tyranny of the Bush administration's usurpations of power and imperialism.

Democracy and freedom cannot endure without the mainstream media holding the government to task, scrutinizing what the government says, and acting with vocal skepticism if the government acts with impunity and willful disregard to voices that disagree with its words and actions. When the mainstream media acts as cheerleader to the administration, it becomes a booster, a propaganda tool of the administration, something we normally associate with despotic rule.

When the Bush administration muffled dissent and accused critics of being unpatriotic, weak on security, and soft on terrorism, and the media reflexively supported whatever was said by that government, the people became the unwitting recipients of the tyranny that befell them.

There is little doubt the mainstream media became a tool of the Bush administration. Instead of balanced reporting of the war, the media gave Americans glorification of the Bush administration's pursuits while fawning at those in power. Early on in the Bush administration, the president held a news conference but only answered questions from a list of preferred journalists (apparently, those who were considered critics of the president were not called upon). Where was the outcry to this blatant staging (managing) of this news conference? Criticism was confined to Internet blogging.

The mainstream media abdicated its responsibility because it feared being branded as unpatriotic and part of the "liberal media." The mainstream media abandoned its role as the natural skeptic of government, becoming, instead, the enabler of the administration's abuses and usurpation of power (ignoring the critics and muting those voices).

It hid behind the façade of objectivity, becoming instead stenographers of whatever pronouncements the administration advanced. A "free" press was reduced, unwittingly or intentionally, to being a propaganda organ of the Bush administration.

Tyranny, the natural enemy of a free people, thrives where propaganda and misinformation is not questioned and the tyrants' lies are not exposed.

It is the role of the mainstream media to be the primary purveyor of keeping the people informed, to uncovering the truth, to exposing falsehoods and lies.

During the time of Watergate, when Bob Woodward of *The Washington Post* was investigating the tentacles of the infamous break-in, his primary informant, later to be known as "Deep Throat," continually admonished Woodward to "follow the money."

Woodward did and, along with his *Post* colleague, Carl Bernstein, uncovered the biggest political cover-up and scandal in the history of this country, up until the time of the Bush administration.

That the Bush administration has received a "pass" and has riden off into the sunset without being held to account for its transgressions, without any justice brought to bear on the culprits, is perhaps one of the largest crimes ever to be perpetrated on the American people by its government. The mainstream media did its part to make this injustice happen.

THE "PHONY" WARS: WAR ON DRUGS, WAR ON TERRORISM

As with Prohibition, and later the War on Crime, the War on Poverty, the War on Drugs, and the War on Terrorism all are contrived "wars" that did nothing to eliminate their root causes.

Declaring "war" on something supposes an intention to mean business. But look at the reality.

Prohibition did nothing to curb alcohol consumption, but it did create a lucrative market for gangsters who controlled the illegal liquor. At least with that "war," sanity prevailed fourteen years later and it was repealed.

As for the "War on Crime," created during the Kennedy era, it produced a few show trials, and some of the higher profile gangsters were sent to prison. When last looked at, crime continues to flourish as ever. This "war" died of neglect.

The "War on Poverty" had good intentions, but trying to eliminate something that has always existed is like trying to eliminate disease. It too died of neglect.

The "War on Drugs" continues to this day, but like alcohol before it, it proliferates with no effect on drug use. It is a big contributor to overall crime and has been a great financial boon to Mafia types. Although billions are poured into this "war" with few gains made, the same approach of legalization (like alcohol) seems nowhere near on the horizon.

The granddaddy of all these phony "wars" is the "War on Terrorism," the brainchild of the Bush administration created after the 9/11 terrorist attacks. This whopper of a lie has the far-reaching implication of establishing endless war.

As clearly stated earlier, terrorism, which has always existed, is a "tactic" used by foes with little or no other means to fight against a more powerful foe. It exists within the indigenous population, inconspicuously in the shadows, creating havoc, chaos, and despair wherever it operates. It cannot be fought with large standing armies, as terrorists (particularly the radically fundamentalist, extremist Muslim Jihadist type) are prepared and committed to go on indefinitely, and armies serve as convenient targets, whose usual response to terrorist attacks is typically overreaction, overwhelming firepower that often results in the killing of innocents, which works to gain sympathy and more adherents for the terrorist cause, which is the exact opposite of what is intended

The "War on Terror," like all these other "wars" mentioned, cannot be won.

Terrorism, like drugs, alcohol, and crime, can be contained. Terrorist acts are criminal, and as with other criminals, to bring terrorists to justice requires tough, hard police work, exchange of intelligence, and cooperation with allies.

With regard to al Qaeda-type terrorism, the U.S. presence in Muslim countries only serves to exacerbate it. This, coupled with the Bush administration's resorting to torture and humiliation in the Iraq War, only broadened the terrorists' allure. In Iraq, however, terrorism was quelled by the local Sunni "awakening,"[22] tribes who turned against terrorism because of the terrorists' excesses in killing innocent Muslims, not the "surge," as reported in the mainstream media.

Terrorism, along with a reconstituted Taliban, is flourishing in Afghanistan, in an area that historically is resistant to any central government control, and along the border of Pakistan. NATO forces have been enlisted to fight it. Sooner or later, fighting an endless, unwinnable war against an enemy that operates in the shadows and is prepared to endure as long as it takes will result in our eventual abandoning of the

---

22 See Chapter7 "Imperialism, Militarism, Foreign Policy, Pre-Emptive War," which explains this phenomenon. Also see Footnote 15.

costly endeavor and retreating (as the British did in the 1800s and the Soviets did in the 1980s).

Fighting phony "wars" with armies is not the same as fighting a necessary, legitimate war against the likes of Nazi Germany and Imperial Japan in World War II.

We have satellite surveillance of all suspected terrorist areas. We have worldwide alliances with governments that view the scourge of terrorism as blight and want it brought under control and contained.

Just as with drugs and crime, terrorism is a problem that exists everywhere in the world. It is only the United States that overreacts, using overheated rhetoric that announces "war" on these things that have always existed and can never be completely eradicated. Yet, the deception continues.

Opposition forces throughout history, when facing an enemy of greater firepower and superior forces, rely on stealth, surprise, ambush, dramatic raids, and all manner of "tactics" to fight its enemy. These forces traditionally have chosen their targets to have the greatest psychological effect on its enemy and to disrupt their "normal" functioning, again to get the greatest dramatic effect.

Terrorists' tactics cannot defeat its larger, more powerful enemy, but its purpose is to wear down the enemy, render the enemy weary, and outlast the enemy until the enemy finally withdraws. This was clearly seen in Vietnam when the North Vietnamese continued its "hit-and-run" tactics, choosing "soft targets" and engaging its enemy on the battlefield only in surprise, which had the most dramatic effect. The "Tet offensive" in 1968 was not a military success (in standard ways of measuring battles won or lost). It did have the effect of causing maximum psychological dislocation (i.e., that it would continue to wage a "shadowy" war as long as it took for its enemy to wear down and tire of losing its men and would finally withdraw).

Today, when terrorists are facing overwhelming firepower, they engage in tactics using anything to gain an advantage.

The terrorist dresses the same way as every other person. The terrorist speaks the same language, is thoroughly familiar with the terrain, and has seemingly unlimited resources and the availability of modern small arms. He moves seamlessly in the midst of the ordinary population, and he chooses the time and place to engage his foe.

The phony "War on Terrorism" must be exposed for what it is. Despite the rhetoric of Osama bin Laden, this is no worldwide, monolithic force capable of destroying and conquering us. Terrorists reign over no country and have no capacity now or in the future for such rule, and like other criminal enterprises, terrorism must be contained and deterred. Its tactic, as old as man himself, will never be eliminated. It must be seen for what it is, not made into something it is not.

As for our "War on Terrorism" in the United States, if we get past the politics of what it is, we would be better off seeing what it is not. It is:

- Not a threat to toppling our democracy

- Not a threat to our institutions (i.e., education, family, religious, commerce, transportation)

- In essence, not a threat to our way of life

Even if an attack is made, the greater harm is more psychological than physical. The American people's attitude should be, regardless of what acts the terrorists commit, it will not change our way of life. We should go about our normal business and refuse to be cowed by their maniacal ways and means. This is not to say we should not take precautions, protect our ports, screen the cargo and other commerce entering the country, keep proper data bases of known terrorists, and monitor their intentions through modern technology and human resources.

But the approach of the Bush administration, essentially scaring our people through warnings and alerts, creates unnecessary fear, anxiety, and/or disbelief when too many cries of wolf turn out to be false.

Terrorism is a containable, controllable menace. It is not the newest monolithic enemy capable of taking over the world. That fallacy, perpetrated and exaggerated by the Bush administration, must be dispelled. It is believed (by some) *only* in the United States and a few others elsewhere in the world.

THE BY-PRODUCTS

A *by-product* can be defined simply as something that occurs as a result of something else happening, which about brings the by-product. Example: Someone experiments with drugs—cocaine or heroin—and, with multiple uses, becomes addicted. The addiction is a by-product brought about by the excessive use of drugs. This addiction may lead to other criminality (robbery), which then becomes a by-product of the drug addiction.

We are a society characterized by much excessive behavior, which leads to many of the negative by-products we see every day.

Obesity has become rampant in our society. It is unclear as to what exactly has created this phenomenon, but its increase is undeniable.

Our manufacturing base is shrinking every year, but it seems one of our growth industries is gambling, particularly casino-type gambling. Of course, most people who gamble in casinos are not addicted, but there is a definite increase in gambling addiction, which is likely a by-product of the increased gambling opportunities available now in many states.

The country's financial system has incurred massive debt, primarily from mortgage loan defaults and the collapse of the housing bubble. Meanwhile, personal debt has accelerated from home equity loans (many of which are part of the current housing default meltdown) coupled with massive credit card debt from overspending and overconsumption. The country is awash in debt, all a by-product of easy credit and governmental deregulation fueled by greed, speculation, and deceptive loan practices of Wall Street.

Our public school systems are not immune to some of the negative by-products that are peculiar to our culture. Our students, besides being lured to identify with corporate culture marketing, are subjected to all manner of by-products just by their attendance in public schools. Some of those by-products are the following:

- Peer pressure to conform to whatever *subculture* predominates in the school, both positive: academic (pre-college) and athletics, and negative: gangs, delinquency, drugs, sex

- Peer pressure to wear clothes conforming with corporate identity

- Bullying, intimidating, ridiculing, and derision

- Addictions (drugs, alcohol, sexual activity, shopping, and eating disorders from overeating to bulimia)

- Depression and suicide

- High dropout rates

We have become a consumer-driven culture enticed to buy and use, often to excess and addiction. The by-products of our corporate-driven marketing has helped to produce some people who are conditioned to be unthinking, uncritical, and irresponsible, molded into becoming excessive consumers and users, who are susceptible to deceptive propaganda, both corporate and politically inspired, that flourishes in this country.

ELECTION 2008

The 2008 run for the presidency was a historic election. No other election in this nation's history was comparable: A black man running, an economy in disarray, an unpopular war droning on endlessly, and the people saying (in polls) the nation was seriously "off-track."

Barack Obama, an articulate, bright black man, captured the imagination of many in America, touching a nerve that captivated his audiences and inspired people to believe he could offer a way out of the present morass.

The contrast between candidates Obama and McCain could not have been starker. Differences between the two candidates included their positions on the war in Iraq, the financial market meltdown, tax cuts for the rich, a recognition of the Bush administration's incompetence on a grand scale, cronyism, corruption, and incredibly, the torture of the detainees (considering McCain's well-known history of himself being tortured at the hands of the North Vietnamese, a position McCain acknowledged in a vote condoning waterboarding). McCain was tied to Bush, and no "maverick" reputation could offset that.

The world was watching. The United States' reputation in the world was never lower. The torture of detainees did that. Sure, outlaw regimes torture. That is to be expected; not so Western democracies. That is a line that had not been crossed, at least not until the Bush administration besmirched the United States' reputation as a moral force in the world with its descent into "dark" territory, authorizing torture and thereby exposing the evil it so loudly proclaimed it was fighting against.

There was much euphoria surrounding the Obama candidacy: A black man, who inspired and offered hope and change. Considering the last seven-plus years of the rogue Bush administration's pre-emptive wars, cronyism, and incompetence on a grander scale than ever witnessed in this country, and with the economy in shambles, it is no wonder so many people connected with a man whose eloquence and authenticity resonated with so many.

There are many critical issues that go to the heart of what plagues this country. Can Obama take on the military industrial complex and the bloated defense industry budget of unnecessary expenditures on armaments that are *unnecessary*, that are built to defend against an enemy that no longer exists? Will Obama seek to curb the influence of corporate lobbying and special interests that corrupt the U.S. legislative process? Can Obama reinstall diplomacy and international cooperation as a centerpiece of foreign policy?

More issues need to be addressed. They include the following:

- The role of deregulation in the financial sector that fostered the rampant speculation and greed by Wall Street, which created the financial meltdown

- The third-rail issue of the Palestinian/Israeli situation with the U.S. biased support tilted toward Israel, preventing any viable solution

- The contrived manifestation of the Bush administration in a "War on Terrorism" that advocated the absurd fighting of terrorism with armies, which exacerbated and expanded terrorism due to the killing of innocents

- The policy of pre-emptive war that got us into Iraq

- The demonization of Iran and the consideration of pre-emptive attack

- The policy of not engaging in diplomacy with adversaries

- The proposed missile defense system in Eastern Europe (which cannot deter a multi headed nuclear attack) against a country (Iran) that does not have existing nuclear bomb capability (but is seen by Russia as directed at them)

- The use of torture on detainees

With America's need to become energy independent and no longer reliant on foreign oil for its energy supply, there has arisen the issue of new offshore drilling for oil along the U.S. coasts, another issue of deception that is nothing more than a con job, as offshore drilling will not affect gas prices. The oil companies have existing leases on millions of acres throughout the country where, presently, they are not drilling.

As for our politics as usual, people knew they were being lied to, even expected it as a matter of course. They say, "What do you expect?" or, "All the politicians do it," or, "That is the way it is," essentially saying nothing could be done about it and dismissing it with cynicism: "What else is new?"

That has not been the case with Barack Obama. He has the charisma that transcends the normal political discourse, inspiring many to believe, and offering them hope.

Obama has connected with young adults normally so turned off by the political process, as most hardly bothered to vote before Obama came on the scene in this election.

In another dark economic time, in the 1930s, and with the country in a deep Depression, FDR invoked, "There is nothing to fear but fear itself." It did not end the Depression, and it did not provide jobs for those without them. But it was the truth, and most people revered the man who said it. FDR was by no means perfect, but the people trusted him, and even though he was a man of wealth and a politician, FDR was considered a man of the people, and they felt he was one of them. Something similar has occurred with the landslide victory of Barack Obama.

Today, with the country facing economic difficulties worse than any time since the 1930s Depression, America has once again turned to another transformational figure, while waiting impatiently for the Bush chapter to close.

PUBLIC FINANCING OF ELECTIONS

America was not always this way. What is occurring today in this country did not happen overnight. There have always been moneyed interests in this country who exploited and used their means to gain the fortunes they amassed, mostly at the expense of other people. That is the way of wealth. By virtue of that wealth, they always have had influence on the government, but they did not control all the reins of power as they do today.

Despite the unique phenomenon of Barack Obama (who refused public financing for his general election campaign, opting instead to continue his Internet-driven fundraising, amply supplemented by big-moneyed contributions, which dwarfed the small donors), there still is no reform needed more than public financing of elections. It surpasses all others for one simple reason: All other real reforms stem directly or indirectly from its implementation.

Simply put, big corporate money and special interests finance the candidates, including Obama, who run for office, making those elected beholden to those interests. The legislative agenda (that is proposed for enactment into law) is determined primarily to favor these interests.

And whether or not that agenda best serves the public interest is rarely a consideration.

The idea of public financing of elections is not a new one. The root cause of "why things are the way they are," has not been seen as a direct result of America's present system of financing elections.

Most politicians in office do not discuss public financing. If they do, public financing has not been their top priority. And why should it be?

For those in office, under the present system, it is in their interest to keep that system as it is. Public financing might seriously undermine their re-election (their primary goal from the day they are elected). Thus, for most of those in office, open advocacy of public financing could clearly jeopardize their staying in office. You would not advocate your own possible demise; neither would most incumbents.

Considering the complicity of our lawmakers, who enacted the deregulation of financial institutions, which unleashed the current American financial system from its moorings and set off the worst economic and financial meltdown since the 1930s Depression, the need for reform of our political system has never been greater.

Although the present economic catastrophe demands some immediate emergency measures, the long-term prognosis for the political and economic stability and well-being of the country requires the overhaul of our present money-dictated electoral system in favor of the basic fundamental reform of public financing of elections.

This necessary endeavor of reforming America will not be easy. The forces against it are formidable, and they will do everything to disgrace and ridicule it as something "un-American," "unpatriotic," against "individual liberty," as something "socialist" that a terrorist would use to undermine America, and even go so far as saying it restricts free speech, guaranteed by the Constitution.

Well, America has been usurped, little by little, by the moneyed interests that are interested only in the power that money bestows upon them.

It is all of one piece, not formally connected, but intertwined with tentacles that reach everywhere in a headlong pursuit to acquire as much money and power through the use of any methods and schemes to garner it, whether it is done ruthlessly or through public relations, by subterfuge or sweet talk, marketed through high-powered lobbying or simple direct corruption, with no concern for any principle other than the pursuits of money and power; and the public interests be damned in the process.

Our present system gives lip service to responding to the people. It is merely window dressing.

We cannot remain disengaged and indifferent, as we had been prior to the federal bailout of Wall Street in October 2008.

History has shown that people can be fooled by propaganda and deceptive marketing, whether corporate or politically inspired. That is, up until the deception is laid bare and the truth is found out. Then the people have to act[23] (as they did recently when the $700 billion federal bailout plan was announced).

The 2006 midterm elections were such a watershed moment. Those Congressional elections were essentially a referendum on George W. Bush, even though Bush was not running. The Democrats regained control of the House and the Senate because the people wanted action to end the war in Iraq. Subsequent events, primarily the intransigence of the Republicans, prevented it from happening. The people were stymied from getting the action they wanted because the system in place prevented it from happening. The system in place could not respond to the people.

There needs to be a return to the concept of the citizen legislator, the idea of one serving his country as opposed to being a career politician. Early in the country's development, politicians had other vocations and continued in them while serving the country. Today, it is rare for a politician on the national scene to be anything else other than a politician once in office.

Term limits were an idea promoted in the eighties as a response to scandals during the Reagan administration. It never took hold, and term limits is hardly mentioned now.

In a system of public financing of elections, serving one's country could make a comeback of sorts. Serving in the public interest is exactly what public financing of elections would promote. One would not be serving to get rich while in office or afterward in the capacity of a lobbyist. And certainly, moneyed special interests would not be the

---

23   *In a rare display of people-driven democracy in action, when the bailout plan for Wall Street was first announced, the public outcry against it, made directly to their own representatives, was extraordinary. Though the plan was eventually passed, it showed that Congress will respond to the people, when they are sufficiently aroused and vocal. The people controlled the agenda, if only for that day.*

primary financial backers of those elected, thus diminishing the hold these interests possess, which corrupts our presently flawed system.

It would also eliminate the need for politicians to continually run for office, as they do now. Their primary focus today is getting elected and then re-elected, which focuses their attention on continually raising money for the next election cycle. Eliminate the need to continually raise money, and the time in office could well be spent representing the people's interest and promoting the people's agenda.

It would have the effect of transforming this country, reigniting a civic spirit that has been crushed by money's influence and the power it commands. This should not be considered a quaint ideal or a belief that all corruption would be eliminated. Men and women are flawed and susceptible. Moneyed interests and corruption will not go away in a system of public financing, but with real enforcement of laws, regulations, and oversight, it could be controlled.

Corrupted politicians will be better held to account and disgraced for betraying the public trust. Now, only the most egregious and brazen are caught. In our present system, reform never gets beyond the tip of the iceberg as it pays lip service to real reform, because a system that has money and special interest influence as its centerpiece cannot be anything but corrupt. When the majority of people say the country is "off-track," they need to know the reasons. In the United States, it is primarily the moneyed and special interests that are at the heart of what is wrong with the power those interests wield.

If legislators are beholden to moneyed and special interests (that bankroll them in office), they may technically reign in office, but the agenda they put forth and the legislation and regulations they enact and enforce are to those benefactors' interest; it is those benefactors who are really in charge.

The people may elect those in office, but they literally only get to choose the candidates that are preselected by the moneyed and special interests. By allowing unlimited money to back candidates these interests preselect, it is a closed system and money reigns supreme.

Barack Obama has seemingly cracked that system with his election. Although Howard Dean used the Internet to finance his 2004 campaign, Obama's success at using the Internet to finance his presidential campaign has been unprecedented.

It remains to be seen if President Obama can initiate policies that can effectively change the system that selects and elects the Congress and most state legislatures. Obama could put in motion a public financing of elections plan by using the "bully pulpit" that he will command. Considering he was selected and elected by the flawed system currently in place, such benevolence would be unprecedented and unlikely, although he has verbally supported public financing in the past.

If a fraction of government spending on unnecessary military hardware (planes, aircraft carriers, submarines, missile defense systems) was eliminated, the money saved could be allocated to rebuild infrastructure, such as repair deteriorating roads, bridges, schools, parks, water treatment systems, and decaying pipes and aquifers that have long been neglected. This would decrease unemployment, but it would also be a positive use of government spending that benefits the public and has a positive return on the money spent.

We have become far removed from our founders' intent of a representative democracy with a republican form of government under the Constitution and following the rule of law, an experiment where the people are sovereign, and government is answerable to the people, with the consent of the people.

Now America has nongovernmental organizations (NGOs), watchdog groups that act in the public interest. These groups don't act in unison, however, as their interests are narrow and specific and have little broad application.

They are like tiny little dogs nipping at the heels of those in power; they can hardly reverse the power structure. They are usually fended off by legal arguments and court delays (often until most of the perpetrators are safely out of office).

Under public financing of all elections and a true people's agenda holding the reins of power, secret dealings and clandestine meetings involving business interests and government officials could be subject to real scrutiny by effective oversight, hearings, and investigations, holding all involved accountable for their actions.

Today, there are occasional Congressional hearings and investigations, but with most elected officials beholden to the moneyed interests they really serve, these elected officials often act with impunity, knowing their involvement in shady dealings will be mostly shielded from real scrutiny, shrouded in a miasma of political puffery, obfuscation, and deception.

As was said earlier, in the case of convicted lobbyist Jack Abramoff (whose corruption and illegal dealings were so openly brazen and surprisingly overt), investigations and convictions were held to a minimum with only those implicated directly forced to resign. As usual, only the tip of the iceberg was revealed. The tentacles that reached to all the levels of moneyed interests and power were never revealed and held to account. Revealing that would implicate the entire power structure. Better to contain it, limit it, have a few show trials, and keep the rest safely under wraps. Revealing the wanton corruption that prevails is not in the existing power structure's interest. Nothing of real consequence is done, and everything goes back to business as usual.

There is little doubt man's activities contribute to global warming and the deterioration of the environment.

In a perfect example of how the agenda of big-moneyed and special interests reign supreme in this country, the Bush administration announced on July 11, 2008, that the 1970 Clean Air Act cannot address climate change and, according to the Environmental Protection Agency, is "ill suited" for correcting global warming, and "it is really at the feet of Congress."

Congress, being the handmaiden of the big-moneyed interests, will do the bidding of these interests and, of course, do nothing. The Bush administration rejected the findings of experts who, unsurprisingly, found greenhouse gases need to be further regulated, as they do contribute to global warming. The administration said that would cripple the U.S. economy. In essence, it would hurt the profits of big-moneyed interests that pollute and despoil the environment and would crimp their further enrichment at the expense of people's health and safety.

With the political agenda controlled lock, stock, and barrel by the big-moneyed interests, the people's interests are guaranteed to go wanting. Instead we get the usual propaganda appeals as the presidential press secretary spouted, "There's a right way and a wrong way to deal with climate change." It is wrong, he said, "to sharply increase gasoline prices, home heating bills, and the cost of energy for American businesses."

Of course, that made it sound like legislation to regulate greenhouse gas would not be in the people's interests and would be "poor for business." The people, of course, were not consulted as to what is in their interests, what their thoughts and ideas are, and what legislation and regulation would be most beneficial to them.

In a Congress elected with public financing, a true people's agenda can be put forth and real legislation and regulation could be enacted to control environmental despoiling. When you are truly beholden to the people, it is the people's interest that would be paramount.

Everything is interconnected. If the people do not understand and see how the present system works *against* the people instead of *for* the people, how can that system be corrected? As was said earlier in this piece, the present power structure will do everything to demonize public financing and prevent it from becoming universal across the country. They have the power. They benefit from this power. They would no longer be in the pinnacle of absolute power.

In all likelihood, only a Constitutional amendment mandating public financing at all governmental levels could fundamentally change the power structure and return the control to the people.

With a publicly financed election process and a true people's agenda in place, a true economic transformation could take place in this country. For example:

- Provide tax incentives to companies operating and manufacturing in the United States

- Eliminate any tax incentive and subsidies to companies that outsource manufacturing jobs to foreign countries

- Commit to rebuilding infrastructure: roads, schools, bridges, levees, water treatment plants, libraries, park lands, museums, recreation facilities, government buildings, public works projects

- Provide tax incentives and tax breaks for alternative energy sources to new start-up companies

- Reduce military expenditures for weapons systems unnecessary against enemies that no longer exist: atomic subs, new generation jets (fighters and bombers), aircraft carriers

- Eliminate "Star Wars"-type missile defense systems (again to defend against enemies that no longer exist)

- Provide health care for everyone with the savings from reduced military expenditures

- Effectively conduct oversight and demand accountability

  - Contain and control corruption with officeholders and lobbyists held accountable

  - Reduce government waste on expenditures

  - Eliminate single-source and no-bid contracts

  - "Sunset" programs that are no longer needed

  - Streamline government (removing and/or reducing overlap functions of agencies)

  - Eliminate pork barrel spending and "earmarks"

  - Eliminate costly programs on phony "wars": crime, drugs, terrorism

  - Reduce prison populations by not incarcerating nonviolent offenders and drug users with violent predators

- Review all security programs and agencies: streamline and eliminate overlap, eliminate the separate Homeland Security Department, and place it in the Justice Department or place it within the FBI

- Eliminate the oil depletion allowance to big oil companies

- Increase taxes on the rich and on excessive profits of corporations

In a government of publicly financed lawmakers, beholden to the public and a public agenda, there would be huge investments in new clean energy technologies such as wind power. These investments could be in the form of tax credits and subsidies to companies that would invest in wind turbine farms that can produce energy on a scale unimaginable just a few short years ago.

This would have the effect of reducing our oil dependency as well as improving the environment. This can occur only through government-sponsored incentives.

The extraordinary profits of big oil produced no benefits to the public, only the pain of higher prices at the pump. Big oil solely benefited from its companies' bottom lines, increased the share value to its investors, and further lined the pockets of their top executives. There are no incentives to do anything other than to continue on our present environmentally destructive course.

Thus, public financing of elections becomes the issue most in need of implementation. The corrupting influence of big money and its power is destroying the fabric of American society more than anything else. Americans have to break the back of this omnipresent cancer by removing the big-moneyed interests from the equation. The country is founded on the principle "of, by, and for the people," not of, by, and for the big corporations, the rich, and the officeholders that benefit and hold office because of big-money largesse that finances their being elected.

"McCain-Feingold" reform of campaign financing was nothing more than a band-aid to be maneuvered around, for it did not eliminate big-money influence and domination from the process. Big money must be excised out of the equation because of its outsized influence on election outcomes. Money dictates, not only who is considered running for office, but once nominated, who gets the most air time, the most exposure, and, therefore, the best chance of being elected.

We must return to the idea of our elected officials being accountable to the people. Representative democracy must mean what it says, not some quaint idea of a bygone era.

Too many Americans do not even bother to vote and are dismissive of the franchise because they believe they have no say in what happens politically, and therefore voting does not matter to them.

Alas, such casual derision helps foster the belief of those in power that the people can be manipulated, distracted, and made fearful. The elected officials continue their mendacious ways, largely unhampered and unaccountable. A Hurricane Katrina happens and the full force of official incompetence and mismanagement hits home harder than the storm itself. Until we change the current system of how we fund our elections, there will continue to be more of the same business as usual. Let us not wonder, "Why?" We have what we have because we have allowed it to happen.

"Democrats divided on ethics overhaul," was the headline of a recent article in *The Baltimore Sun*. Let us call it the "*dance* around ethics overhaul."

Republicans paid the price in the 2006 midterm elections partly for their outrageous ethics violations, which Democrats rightly coined as a "culture of corruption."

Republicans, however, did not invent the type of lobbying/ Congressional cabal of influence peddling and payoffs that finally caught up with the likes of convicted Republican Congressman "Duke" Cunningham, Bob Ney, and Tom De Lay, who resigned under a cloud of allegations. Democrats, too, when they held majority power in the Congress, resorted to their own ethics violations, perhaps not on as grand a scale.

The "dance" occurs precisely because of the underlying cause, which is money, as many are on the take, directly or indirectly.

The moneyed interests are then reciprocated by elected officials they helped elect through sweetheart deals, legislation, deregulation, tax breaks, favors, influence, and other assorted skullduggery that favors the moneyed interests. The public interest becomes an afterthought to most of our elected officials (unless the public becomes so alarmed they make it known).[24]

An example was the "port security" deal with a Middle Eastern company from the United Arab Emirates, which wanted to buy the port unloading facilities in a number of American cities along the Eastern seaboard of the United States. When the public became aware of the pending deal, they openly complained to Congress, which quickly scuttled the deal.

The only way for public financing of elections to take hold as *the* necessary reform is for the public to demand it. Were Congress to ignore the will of the people, if that will (of the people) clamors for public financing of elections, the people can force it to happen.

The present system must be rejected and replaced with one that can respond to the people. That can only happen with publicly financed elections.

That is why it is the key reform before any other.

The people must see the connection of money and the political process, in the simplest of terms. Response to interests of the people can happen *only* when those they elect are beholden to the people, not our present system, which has those elected beholden to the moneyed and special interests.

Even if the men who drew up the Constitution were flawed, their ideas were sound and high-minded. If reality betrays the truth that we have not yet achieved these ideals, it does not make them less worthy of striving to attain them.

---

24   *See Footnote 23 of this chapter.*

Public financing of elections must be recognized by the American people as *the* vehicle that has to be implemented for the political process to change in favor of the public interest.

Big money's impact must be blunted. It will not happen voluntarily or with any half measures that continue to allow big money to reign over the political process.

And it must be universal; all elections—federal, state, and local— must have public financing and be the law of the land.

That is why, in the end, a Constitutional amendment may be the only way for this to happen.

It is the American people who have to be brought to the realization that public financing of elections is the key issue that has to be implemented in order for this Republic to be returned to the people. That without this key element, universally accepted and implemented, this country will remain in the interests of the rich and powerful to do as they please, and the people will remain in bondage to those interests.

Again, we must try to envision a scenario of the political system under public financing.

Big money's influence would no longer determine the agenda. When our officials are not beholden to big money underwriting them, the public interest will shape and determine the political agenda.

Real problem solving could occur, as competency would replace cronyism to fix things. Hurricane Katrina's devastation would not have occurred. The levees that broke would have been built to withstand a category 4 storm. Thus, the flooding that inundated the city would not have occurred. People dying and being displaced would not have happened. Full mobilization of human and material resources would have been brought to bear *before* the hurricane hit. "Browny, you are doing a heckuva job," would not have been mouthed by a clueless president. Somebody competent would have been in charge, connected to all first responders in a coordinated and organized fashion.

What occurred in New Orleans is unconscionable, but it was all but foreordained. Our system is built to fail. It has little chance to succeed. Our true problems are hardly ever faced, let alone discussed. Incompetence and cronyism prevail.

Our economy would not be in the shape that it is in. The banking and finance industry would be properly overseen and regulated. The schemes and financial skullduggery would not have been permitted. The mortgage loan crisis would not have been allowed to occur. Fannie Mae and Freddie Mac would be wholly public institutions, not semi-private, with their lobbyists walking the corridors of Congress and represented on the stock market exchange. They would exist strictly in the public interest and not to the benefit of its executives, who joined in the deregulated free-for-all of greed and wild speculation that forced the Treasury bailout.

What is required is a fully formed public financing requirement at every level: local, state, and federal.

Again, as the chances are slim that legislation will be enacted, it may require a Constitutional amendment to be passed to cleanse our system, especially if, as expected, the Supreme Court rejects full public financing as an infringement of free speech. Therefore, the law of the land may require this change in the Constitution.

Then our country will be returned to the people, ending our present system that reigns to the benefit of the wealthy few and to the detriment of the rest of us.

It is the indispensable sine qua non of political reforms.

It would require a massive outpouring of people, NGOs, churches, the Red Cross, the ACLU, the Internet, and public financing spokesmen able to educate the broad spectrum of people in understanding the necessity and why this will bring about the changes that are so necessary. Our country's survival as a free, democratic Republic may depend on it.[25]

25 *It is fully acknowledged that President Barack Obama has advocated many of the changes recommended in these pages. It remains to be seen whether he, even with a Democratically controlled Congress, can pull it off. It is sincerely hoped that he will. If hedoes not, the reasons may well be found in the flawed political system that exists and requires the changes recommended in these pages.*

EPILOGUE

The Constitution of the United States starts with, "We the people," not the president, not the Congress, not the Supreme Court, but "We the people."

Barack Obama has energized the country. He won despite the corrupt system. Can he really change it with the rest of government and big-moneyed interest's influence still in place? Or will the changes just be incremental, piecemeal, around the edges? The heart of the problem is the outsized influence that big-moneyed interests exert on the political process and its agenda. It was money that contributed to his victory. Certainly it was more than that. He did receive mountains of money from those big-moneyed interests in the general election campaign. Traditionally, that has meant embracing the agenda of those interests over the people's interests. Will that change? Much is unknown. In the presidential campaign, the present system precluded discussion of many critical issues facing the country. Two of those issues were the bloated defense budget and America's biased relationship toward Israel. The former has been a sacrosanct totem, while the latter has been a third rail. Many of the conflicts in the Muslim world have the Israeli/Palestinian problem at their core, and much of the terrorism in that part of the world is connected with the Israeli occupation. A viable two-state solution must be achieved.

The defense budget is unjustified relative to the type of adversaries we face. Money is spent unnecessarily against a foe that no longer exists. This is absurd on its face. The defense budget requires serious reduction so those funds can go to rebuilding American infrastructure, developing new energy resources, and keeping industry from leaving the country. War making should not be what we are about.

Financial regulations in banking and finance must be reinstituted, reining in the greedy speculation that was at the heart of the current meltdown.

Pure, unfettered capitalism is a myth; allowed to function unregulated, it always results in financial ruin and economic calamity. When the government capitalists abhor is required to come to the rescue to keep the country from total collapse, this is a form of socialism. It is nationalism, when the government takes over the banks. That is the reality. You solve problems facing reality, not avoiding that reality. Let us not pretend the necessary government entry into business is unnecessary. Let us accept it, embrace it, and encourage it, not hold our nose, disparage it, and bail out business so it can return to its speculative, greedy nature when the dust settles from the latest calamity it perpetuated.

So it is, up and until the phenomenon of Barack Obama.

The American people have not been vigilant in preserving the experiment started some 232 years ago, failing to hold to account those who would destroy and corrupt the fabric of the country. We Americans have let the power and influence of big-moneyed and special interests undermine and rig the political process. The system that has evolved is corrupt to its core and is close to being unredeemable. The American people permit this business as usual at the peril of their free, open, and democratic society.

So, what of the people in this country? It is "ours" as much as "theirs." Are the American people condemned to be spectators rather than active participants to the drama happening around them, like Nero, fiddling while Rome burned? Are the American people too disengaged, disinterested, and unaffected, unable to summon the necessary energy or even the desire to correct their failing system?

Some people seem oblivious and unaware, unable even to identify the "fire," much less the "smoke." Others are too cynical or beaten down, the life run out of them. But what of those saddened by what they see; will they pick up the challenge?

The George W. Bush administration represents the natural consequence of the slow erosion of our Constitutional representative democracy, which has been usurped in favor of the dominance of big money and special interests ruling our political process. They "own" it, and they reign over it. The "people's" representatives have become big money's agents, who remain the people's representatives in name only. The political agenda, the laws and regulations enacted, and the actions taken reveal who truly owns the country.

We, the American people, have all but forfeited our freedom and democracy by not being vigilant, as this erosion, in our name, has been allowed to happen.

This is the clear implication of what now is so prominent and represented by the financial and economic meltdown that is currently ravaging the country.

We, the American people, have been builders. We have had a strong work ethic. We have been achievers, producers, innovators, developers, initiators. Progress has been in our blood. We have excelled at problem solving.

We need to reassess our displaced capabilities that have become warped by greed and rampant speculation (those nefarious activities that have corrupted our system).

The United States has pursued an imperialist path, antagonizing the world, following policies of neo-conservative fantasy of pre-emptive war, misusing America's power while demonizing those who disagree with those policies, as so disastrously evident in the George W. Bush administration. The United States has strained relations with natural allies (who have been denigrated by the Bush administration whenever they part from his neo-conservative policies).

The United States has lost its clarity and the nobility of its purpose. The United States does not need to have its footprint everywhere, to exercise hegemony everywhere in the world. The United States has incurred resentment and fueled the antagonism against us by the "War on Terrorism" that Bush initiated.

The United States must recognize we are a part of the world, not its exclusive owner. America cannot dictate, nor should it expect the world to be like (or even want to be like) the United States. This is hubris, a false assumption that the United States must dispel.

Our political system is fundamentally flawed. If it is allowed to prevail as it presently exists, nothing can change.

The old adage, "Power corrupts, and absolute power corrupts absolutely," accurately depicts our present system. It does not have to be this way.

In poll after poll, the American people have indicated that the country is "off-course." There is hardly any unanimity in the specifics of what constitutes "off-course" other than the listing of the economy, war in Iraq, tax cuts for the rich, financial markets crisis, skewed income distribution, excessive oil profits, the high price of gas, illegal immigration, the "War on Terrorism," and outsourcing of jobs (to list some of the more high-profile issues).

Just like the Supreme Court's inability to define pornography—"You know it when you see it"—the same goes for the country being seriously "off-course." Ask the guy who lost his job after thirty years of working for a company when that company shut down local operations and moved it overseas, or the single parent who works two jobs, has no health insurance, has two children, and struggles to pay the rent and put food on the table. If she gets sick, they may be one step from homelessness.

Yet there is no single factor that one could put his finger on that explains why the country is "off-course." The primary reason is all these things are looked at in isolation, separate from one another. What exists is a *systemic problem*.

Unlike World War II, where there was need for collective action and a specific purpose (do everything to defeat the enemy), Americans now live in a different time, a different era. There are no Nazi Germanys, Imperial Japans, or Soviet Unions. China is one of our largest trading partners (albeit mostly one-sided in their favor), Japan is our ally, Germany is a part of the European Union (its imperialist past dead with Hitler). Despite Russia's ill-proportioned response to Georgia's attack on a wayward province, Russia isn't threatening a new cold war and (though more autocratic than democratic) is no longer a threat to world stability.

Yes, there is terrorism with bin Laden holed up in the mountains in Pakistan, issuing his occasional videos denouncing the United States as Satan. There is President Ahmadinejad of Iran denouncing Israel and denying the Holocaust. There is the seemingly intractable Israeli/Palestinian problem (just as Kashmir is with India and Pakistan). There are the Mugabes of the world, the military junta in Burma, all desperate to retain their power, but hardly a threat to the world.

In reality, there is no real, imminent threat to world peace. None, except us! The United States is the only superpower. The United States is the only country that has military bases all over the world. The United States is the only one that has declared it will go to war pre-emptively. There are no antagonists in the world that are capable of threatening the United States, now or in the foreseeable future. There just are not any! Terrorists with box cutters may have been able to hijack some airplanes and destroy two big buildings in New York, and crash into the Pentagon, but this was hardly the opening salvo to a new world war, a threatening menace to the United States or the world.

The world changed when the cold war ended with the unexpected demise of the Soviet Union. In the absence of this threat, the United States stands alone as the preeminent power. But it is the United States that has yet to reconcile its place in this new world, short of initiating the unnecessary war in Iraq and threatening Iran. It is the United States that has become the primary destabilizing entity in the world.

The Bush administration has committed the United States to an endless "War on Terrorism." The United States has defense expenditures equal to all other countries combined in the world. The United States is the greatest arms supplier in the world, with its presence (with bases) all over the world.

It is the United States that is on a permanent war footing against an enemy that has no standing army or navy, no air force, no weaponry beyond small arms, no missiles, and no capabilities to use them. The United States, with no real imminent threats, now or for the foreseeable future, has created the "illusion" of a threat to justify our enormous bloated defense industry expenditures (yet with no antagonist to use them against).

Thus the heart and soul of our country's being "seriously off-track" is our *inability* to face reality as it actually exists.

If the United States is chasing the chimera of illusionary enemies, how is it able to see and correct the real problems that plague America, that contribute to the current economic trauma, which cause Americans to feel the country is "seriously off-track"?

Hurricane Katrina devastated New Orleans. The problem was known; nothing was done. In contrast, Holland, a country below sea level, has a series of dikes and embattlements to protect it from the worst storms. It planned and carried out the necessary projects to protect its country and its people. Here, we knew of the problem and did nothing to correct it.

The United States has more than 50 million people uninsured. No other first world country has this problem. All have universal coverage for their people. We have no such system.

The manufacturing base of this country has shrunken, its middle class numbers declining, infrastructure deteriorating, a national debt in the trillions (and growing daily), an economic mortgage debt crisis, energy costs escalating, personal credit card debt in the trillions (while personal savings and retirement accounts are rifled), a disparity in wealth (between the richest and poorest) mirroring the age of the "robber barons" in the late nineteenth century.

The United States constitutes 5 percent of the world's population and consumes a third of the world's resources.

To solve our problems will require Americans to face our problems squarely, while determining a course for action. Our problems are *systemic*.

War is profitable to the large corporate special interests and the military/industrial complex. But enemies are needed to conduct war.

With no real "enemies," our leaders contrive them and magnify their menace with falsehoods and propaganda to justify our being on a continued and endless war footing.

The United States is deceptively controlled and manipulated by forces that may appear benign and benevolent, but are gradually undermining and destroying it, all in the name of the people.

The American military does its duty. It is trained, ready, and prepared to defend the country. They are the blunt instrument on "duty" to deter would-be aggressors and, if need be, use that lethal force against those aggressors that do attack the United States.

Attacking Afghanistan in the aftermath of the 9/11 attacks was justified, as the evidence was clear and undeniable that al Qaeda was responsible and they were harbored in Afghanistan by the Taliban government. Attacking Iraq under the pretexts and false pretences was unjustified and never should have been initiated.

Iraq was contained. It was a threat to no other country. The misuse of the American military unnecessarily was an unforgivable act of arrogant power.

When this life-and-death decision was made (and make no mistake, going to war is such a decision), those who made those decisions were not held to account.

As for the issue of deterrence in preventing a nuclear exchange, deterrence works. No nuclear power has ever attacked another nuclear power. It is a primary reason countries want to acquire nuclear arms: to deter potential nuclear aggressors.

Nuclear arms are not an offensive weapon.

Naming Iraq, Iran, and North Korea as the "axis of evil" had no basis in fact and only resulted in Iran and North Korea urgently "ramping up" their fledgling nuclear programs.

The aggressive U.S. actions, particularly in Iraq, have ignited fears, especially of the authoritarian-ruled countries of Iran and North Korea, who believed they were next in the U.S. "sights." Consequently, in response to the American pre-emptive invasion of Iraq, they went after the one weapon that is the deterrent against a pre-emptive attack: their own nuclear arsenal.

Instead of acting as a mature, self-confident adult in the world (not threatened by any power), the United States has become the world's primary belligerent power.

So what has been done in these pages? Written a polemic? Made a clarion call? Sounded the alarm? Made a plea?

An argument has been made that is a critique of what's happening in this country.

If we, Americans, do not act, but allow things to continue (business as usual), permit ourselves to be ruled by the forces we should have brought under our control, we will be complicit to whatever befalls us.

Franklin said, "A Republic, if you can keep it." He knew, one day we could be in danger of losing it.

We have not been vigilant in defending our liberty. We have acquiesced and let power and money usurp our Constitution.

The Bush administration did not start the usurpation of power, eviscerating the Constitution; they have just expanded it.

Comedian George Carlin was completely irreverent, a true iconoclast, identifying, exposing, and skewering the people and institutions that run this country. As he said of money and power, "It is an exclusive club and you're not in it."

Carlin described himself as "disappointed and disillusioned," but as the true patriot he was, he loved his country, he was saddened by the excesses that defiled it. Carlin spoke the truth.

Our American system has been corrupted by a minority of powerful moneyed forces that have seized control of all the mechanisms of power.

Those forces must be identified and exposed, and then the means applied to return the power to the people so the country can be brought closer to its original intent: "of, by, and for the people."

Our governmental system can be reformed, but only if the people demand it.

Except for the chapter recommending public financing of elections, whether one agrees with the many ideas set forth in these pages is not important.

A true democratic republic is messy, but it allows for the many disparate voices to be heard. To flourish, those voices must be given the opportunity to be expressed in a people's agenda, set forth in the people's Houses, by the true representatives of those people.

This can only occur when there is an even playing field, not slanted in favor of those that have so corrupted our American system.

Once again, as Franklin warned, "…a Republic, if we can keep it."

www.ingramcontent.com/pod-product-compliance
Lightning Source LLC
Chambersburg PA
CBHW020255290526
45784CB00003B/1266